THE UK
NINJA Foodi
Recipe Book

Easy and Affordable British Recipes
using Metric Measurements

Introduction

This Ninja foodi cookbook combines the speed and ease of Ninja foodi® cooking to get you preparing delicious food in no time.

Have you ever used Ninja foodi® before? Everything you need to know about cooking in Ninja foodi is included in the easiest-to-follow Ninja foodi cookbook ever. Discover how perfectly cooking and the Ninja foodi® go together. I'm glad you are here, I'm excited to share with you how it can be so easy to make a great food at home in no time. Lets get started.

Contents

- Introduction
- Ninja Foodi 101
- Breakfast & Sides
- Beef & Poultry Mains
- Seafood Mains
- Soups & Stews
- Desserts

Like a microwave or an electric kettle, the Ninja Foodi has become a kitchen staple. it shown us just how quickly it can cook a hearty meal.

Whether you're a new Ninja Foodi owner or it's long been stored away in a cabinet, this guide is for you, it`ll guide you through the basics, including explaining those strange buttons .

To kick things off, let's walk through Ninja Foodi basics. Let's get started.

What is the Ninja Foodi?

It is a type of pressure cooker. It also sautés, slow cooks, steams, crisps, air fry vegetables and poultry, and makes rice. Because it's an all-in-one device, you can brown a chicken and cook it all in the same pot. Most Ninja Foodi meals are ready to serve in under an hour.

What can be cooked with the Ninja Foodi?

In less than 30 minutes, you can prepare a hearty meal for the entire family using the Ninja Foodi. Rice & chicken, beef stew, chili, and even a whole-roasted chicken can be prepared in 30 to 60 minutes. And, yes, the Ninja Foodi can be used to bake bread.

Guide On How To Use The Ninja Foodi

How you use the Ninja Foodi depends on what you'll cook. However, many recipes in this book tend to follow this formula:

1. Turn the Ninja Foodi to Sauté mode and add the oil.

2. When the oil is hot brown the beef/chicken & the garlic/onion.

3. press CANCEL & Deglaze the pot.

4. Close & secure the lid with valve in seal position.

5. Press Manual, then Pressure. Tap it again to go into High Pressure mode (or press Pressure Cook on duo plus model), Use the plus and minus buttons to set the cook time.

6. When the cook time is up, release the pressure. **The pressure can be released in two ways.**

- **Natural pressure release:** the valve on the lid stays in Sealing position and the pressure dissipates naturally over time.
- **Quick Release (Manual Release)** : move the valve into Venting position and let the steam shoots out, releasing the pressure.

What all the buttons on your Ninja Foodi mean?

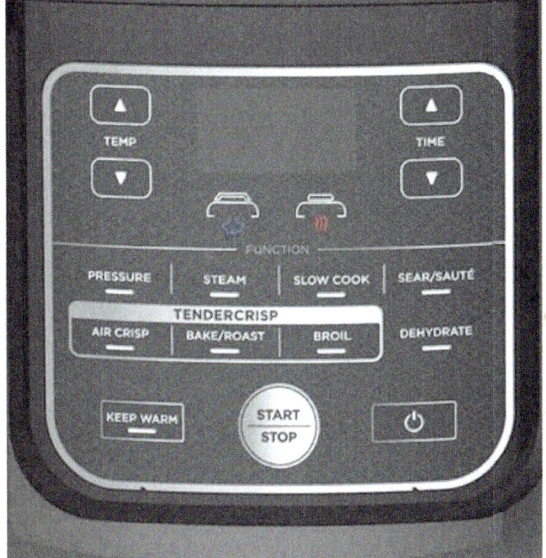

HERE ARE THE MOST USED KEYS IN THIS BOOK RECIPES.

 **Sear/Sauté :** It allows you to brown meats and precook vegetables. You can also use it to thicken sauces or stir fry.

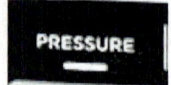 **Pressure Cooking :** These are probably the most used keys. The default pressure setting is High; however, by pressing the Pressure button, you can change the pressure from High to Low. Adjust the pressurized cooking time with the Plus and Minus buttons.

 **TEMP/TIME arrows:** Use the up and down TEMP arrows to adjust the cook temperature and/or pressure level. Use the up and down TIME arrows to adjust the cook time.

 **AIR CRISP:** To use the Ninja Foodi as an air fryer to give foods crispiness and crunch with little to no oil.

SAFETY TIPS EVERY NINJA FOODI OWNER SHOULD KNOW

 Always add at least 1/2 cup of liquid.

 Make sure the lid valve is set to Sealing.

 Before cooking, always double-check that the sealing ring is properly positioned under the lid, clean, and debris-free.

 Stay away from the steam, do not place any exposed body part over the steam valve.

 Be sure to keep your Ninja Foodi out of the reach of children.

Must Have Ninja Foodi Accessories

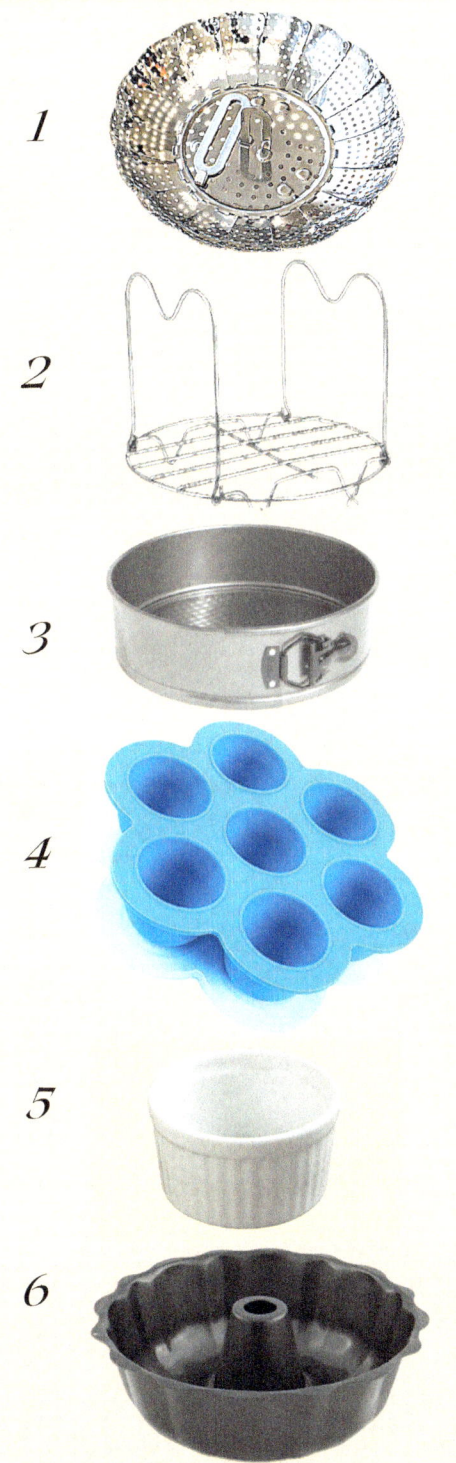

1 Steamer Basket

One of the most basic Ninja Foodi inserts is a metal steamer basket. This simple steamer basket is ideal for cooking vegetables in the Instant Pot.

2 Trivet with Handles

Allows you to remove food quickly without being exposed to hot steam for an extended period of time.

3 Springform Pan

With the springform pan you can make all kinds of Baked foods including cheesecakes and cakes in your Ninja Foodi pressure cooker.

4 Silicone Egg Molds

You can use silicone egg molds to make egg bites, egg muffins, Cupcakes and some other desserts.

5 Ramekins

They are perfect for making pudding and lava cake, 6 oz. ramekins are the size to use for the best results.

6 Tube/Bundt Cake Pan

Can be used to make all kinds of beautiful cakes and also meatloaf.

INDEX

BREAKFAST & SIDES

Breakfast Gravy	1
Egg Salad	2
Deviled Eggs	3
Potato Salad	4
Courgette Pizza Boats	5
Breakfast Pizza	6
Cheese & Bean Quesadillas	7
Breakfast Casserole	8
Grilled Cheese	9
low-Carb Breakfast Casserole	10
Baked Potato	11
Jojo potato wedges	12
Mashed Potatoes	13
Cheesy Garlic Bread	14
Mushroom Pies	15
Courgette Fries	16
Cajun Seasoned Sweet Potato	17
Sweet Potato Fries	18
Green Bean Casserole	19
Air Fried Vegetables	20
Honey Butter Cornbread	21
Cauliflower Fried Rice	22
Mexican Rice	23
Lemon & Parmesan Orzo	24
Buttered Noodles	25

BREAKFAST & SIDES

Mac & Cheese **26**
Penne Pomodoro **27**
Creamy rigatoni **28**
Lemon Garlic Pasta with Vegetables **29**

BEEF & POULTRY MAINS

Chicken Fajitas	31
Chicken Teriyaki Rice	32
Butter Chicken	33
Chicken Stir Fry	34
Greek Chicken wrap	35
BBQ Chicken Legs	36
Sweet & Sour Chicken	37
Crisped Whole Chicken	38
Chicken Pot Pie	39
Cornish Hens	40
chicken Souvlaki	41
Chicken Drumsticks	42
Stuffed Chicken Breasts	43
Onion Chicken	44
Ahead Shredded Chicken	45
Chicken Pad Thai	46
Chicken Chili	47
Chicken Alfredo	48
Picadillo	49
Southwestern Chili	50
Beef Stew	51
Beef Roast	52
Meatloaf	53
Beef Stew with Mushrooms	54
Meatballs	55
Steak Bites	56

BEEF & POULTRY MAINS

Swiss Steak	57
Corned Beef with Cabbage & Potatoes	58
Beef Pot Pie	59
Steak and Vegetable Bowl	60
Scotch Egg	61
Beef And Cabbage	62
Ground Beef And Rice	63
Beef Stroganoff	64
Taco Pasta	65
Hamburger Helper	66
Spaghetti	67

SEAFOOD MAINS

Prawn Fajitas	69
Fish & chips	70
Crab Cakes	71
Grilled Prawn	72
Creamy Cayenne Prawns	73
Seafood Bisque	74
Thai Poached Salmon	75

SOUPS & STEWS

Cabbage Sausage Soup	77
Chicken Enchilada Soup	78
Creamy Mushroom Soup	79
Cheesy Cauliflower Soup	80
Yellow Pea Soup	81
Cullen Skink	82
Minestrone Soup	83
Chicken Noodle Soup	84
Leek & Potato Soup	85
Cheesy Potato Soup	86

DESSERTS

Apple Butter 88
Flan 89
Eggy Bread 90
Lemon Curd 91
Pumpkin Oatmeal 92
Brownies 93
Cookies 94
Raspberry & Orange Bread Pudding 95
Cheesecake 96
Mini Lemon Pies 97
Apple Crumble 98
Rice Pudding 99
Blackberry Cobbler 100
Strawberry Scones 101
Biscuits 102
Bread Pudding 103
Banana Bundt Cake 104
Strawberry Rhubarb Crumbles 105
Shortbread Cookies 106
Blueberry muffin 107

1

Breakfast & Sides

Serving Size
4 Servings

Total Time
15 Minutes

BREAKFAST GRAVY

Ingredients

- **450g ground breakfast sausage**
- **2 tbsp butter**
- **250ml chicken stock**
- **75g plain flour**
- **650ml milk**
- *4 plain scones*
- **Salt & pepper to taste**

Directions

1. Turn the foodi in "Sauté" mode. Add oil. Once hot, add sausage, crumble the sausage and sauté until browned.
2. Add in chicken stock, butter. Stir until combined.
3. Secure lid with valve in seal position. Cook on High pressure for 5 minutes. When time is up, do a quick release.
4. In a large mixing bowl, mix flour and milk until fully combined.
5. Open the lid Turn the foodi in "Sauté" mode. Add flour and milk mixture, season with salt & pepper. stir until thickened for about 5 minutes. Serve over scones.

Per Serving: 580kcal
Fat: 38g, Carbohydrates: 21g, Protein:25g

Serving Size
6 Servings

Total Time
25 Minutes

EGG SALAD

Ingredients

- *6 eggs*
- *250ml water*
- *115g light/regular mayonnaise*
- *1/2 tsp. dill*
- *1/2 tsp. smoked paprika*
- *Salt & pepper to taste*

Directions

1. Add 250ml water to bottom of the ninja. Place Trivet. Add Eggs
2. Secure lid with valve in seal position. Cook on high for 5 minutes. When time is up, let the pressure release naturally for 5 minutes, then do a quick release.
3. Put eggs into ice water for 5 minutes.
4. Peel the eggs and put them into a large bowl. Use a fork to mash the eggs.
5. Add the mayonnaise, dill, paprika, and season with salt & pepper. Mix until all combined.
6. Serve it cold over lettuce or bread.

Per Serving: 120kcal
Fat: 9g, Carbohydrates: 7g, Protein: 6g

Serving Size
24 Servings

Total Time
2 Hours 14 Minutes

DEVILED EGGS

Ingredients

- *12 eggs*
- *250ml water*
- *60g mayonnaise*
- *½ Tsp Dill*
- *1 tbsp sweet relish*
- *1 tbsp smoked paprika*

Directions

1. Add water to bottom of the Ninja Foodi pot. Place Trivet. Add Eggs
2. Secure lid with valve in seal position. Cook on high pressure for 5 minutes. When time is up, wait for 5 minutes, then Do a quick release.
3. Keep the Eggs in Cold water for 5 minutes. Peel the eggs and slice in half.
4. In a small mixing bowl, place the yolks. Add in the mayo, dill, and sweet relish. Mix until combined.
5. Put it in the fridge for 1-2 hours to chill before filling the egg whites.
6. Spoon it into each egg white.
7. Before serving sprinkle with paprika.

Per Serving: 71kcal
Fat: 8g, Carbohydrates: 1g, Protein: 3g

Serving Size
8 Servings

Total Time
33 minutes

POTATO SALAD

Ingredients

- *1.3kg potatoes, (peeled & cut into 2cm cubes)*
- *6 large eggs*
- *100g celery, (chopped)*
- *1 small onion, (chopped)*
- *150g chopped Pickled cucumber*
- *1 tbsp pickle juice*
- *300g mayonnaise*
- *1 tbsp Dijon mustard*
- *½ tsp paprika*
- **Salt & pepper to taste**

Directions

1. Add 1 1/2 cup of water to the bottom of the Ninja pot and season with salt. Place Trivet. Place the steamer basket on the trivet.
2. Add potato cubes, then add the eggs on the potatoes.
3. Secure lid with valve in seal position. Cook on high pressure for 3 minutes, when time is up, let the pressure release naturally for 15 minutes, then do a quick release.
4. Open lid, Remove potatoes and eggs from ninja foodi, let them cool slightly.
5. Peel and chop eggs.
6. In a large bowl, add potato cubes, chopped eggs, celery, onion, and pickle & pickle juice. Mix until combined.
7. Add mayonnaise, paprika and mustard. Mix well. Season with salt and pepper. Serve.

Per Serving: 420kcal
Fat: 27g, Carbohydrates: 39g, Protein:6g

Serving Size
4 Servings

Total Time
15 Minutes

COURGETTE PIZZA BOATS

Ingredients

- **2 Courgettes, (cut lengthwise)**
- **60g Pizza Sauce**
- **Mini Pepperoni**
- **Shredded Mozzarella Cheese**
- **Olive Oil Spray**

Directions

1. Core the courgette middle out with a spoon. Spray the courgette with cooking spray.
2. Brush the courgette with pizza sauce, top with pepperoni and cheese. Put them in the Ninja foodi. Coat them with cooking spray.
3. Air crisp at 180C for 8 minutes. Repeat if necessary for the additional courgette.

Per Serving: 61kcal
Fat: 4g, Carbohydrates: 3g, Protein:3g

Serving Size
6 Slices

Total Time
30 Minutes

BREAKFAST PIZZA

Ingredients

For the Pizza Dough

- *120g all purpose flour*
- *1 tbsp. granulated sugar*
- *1 tsp baking powder*
- *1/8 tsp salt*
- *150g Greek yogurt*
- *12 egg white*

For the Toppings

- *4 slices Beef bacon, cut into thin strips*
- *4 large eggs, beaten*
- *60g cream cheese, room temp*
- *60g freshly shredded cheese*

Directions

1. In a large mixing bowl, add flour, sugar, baking powder, and salt. Mix everything together, add yogurt and mix until form a ball of dough.
2. Use a rolling pin to stretch the pizza dough out into a 20cm round. Brush the top with egg whites.
3. Spray ninja foodi pot/pasket with cooking spray, add pizza to the basket.
4. Air crisp at 190°C for 10 mins, then flip and air fry for more 3 mins.
5. In a skillet over medium-high heat. Add bacon strips and cook. Once cooked, remove skillet from heat and add eggs. Mix & add cream cheese once eggs are nearly cooked. Set aside.
6. Add bacon/eggs mixture to pizza crust. Top with shredded cheese and air crisp for 5 mins until cheese melted and bubbly.

Per Serving: 220kcal
Fat: 13g, Carbohydrates: 17g, Protein:13g

Serving Size
4 Servings

Total Time
20 Minutes

CHEESE & BEAN QUESADILLAS

Ingredients

- 1/2 tbsp. olive oil
- 4 spring onions, (chopped)
- 1 red pepper, (chopped)
- 1 400g tin black beans, (rinsed & drained)
- 200g corn kernels
- 2 tbsp. tomato puree
- 4 tbsp. water
- 1/2 tsp. ground cumin
- 1/2 tsp. paprika
- Salt & pepper to taste
- 4 tortillas
- 120g grated cheddar cheese

Directions

1. In a large pan over medium heat. Heat oil, add the spring onion and pepper, fry for 2 min. Add beans, tomato puree, corn, water, cumin, paprika and season with salt & pepper. Cooking for 3 min.
2. Divide the bean mixture over 4 tortillas, spread it only on half of each tortilla, sprinkle the cheese over the beans
3. Fold over the other half of the tortillas, gently pressing down. Place them on grill rack in the foodi.
4. Put the foodi in the air crisp option at 180c for 3 minutes each side.
5. Serve with salsa.

Per Serving: 380kcal
Fat: 14g, Carbohydrates: 50g, Protein: 20g

Serving Size
6 Servings

Total Time
8 Hours 10 Minutes

BREAKFAST CASSEROLE

Ingredients

- *12 large eggs*
- *250ml milk*
- *900g bag hashed brown potatoes, (slightly thawed)*
- *900g cooked breakfast sausage*
- *150g bell peppers, (chopped)*
- *4 green onions, (chopped)*
- *225g shredded cheddar cheese*
- *2 tsp Dijon mustard*
- *Cooking spray*
- *Salt & pepper to taste*

Directions

1. Spray the bottom of Ninja pot with cooking spray.
2. In a large mixing bowl, Whisk eggs, milk, mustard, salt & pepper until combined. Set aside.
3. Add hashed brown potatoes to the bottom of Ninja pot, layer half the meat, peppers, onion, and 1 cup of cheese on top of the hash browns. Repeat the layers. Pour the egg mixture on top.
4. Secure lid with valve in seal position. Cook on low for 7-8 hours.
5. Serve immediately.

Per Serving: 520kcal
Fat: 30g, Carbohydrates: 8g, Protein: 25g

 **Serving Size** 2 Servings

 **Total Time** 10 Minutes

GRILLED CHEESE

Ingredients

- **4 slices bread**
- **4 slices cheese**
- **2 tbsp butter softened (or mayo)**

Directions

1. Preheat Ninja foodi at 200C
2. Butter outside of bread, placing 2 slices of cheese in the middle of each sandwich.
3. Air crisp for 3 minutes on each side.

Per Serving: 477kcal
Fat: 25g, Carbohydrates: 28g, Protein:15g

Serving Size 8 Servings **Total Time** 25 Minutes

LOW-CARB BREAKFAST CASSEROLE

Ingredients

- *450g ground sausage*
- *1 onion, (chopped)*
- *1 green bell pepper, (chopped)*
- *8 eggs, (beaten)*
- *60g shredded Colby/Monterey Jack cheese*
- *1/2 tsp. garlic salt*
- *Cooking spray*

Directions

1. Turn the ninja in "Sauté" mode, brown the sausage. Add onion and bell pepper, cook along until onion is soft and the sausage is cooked.
2. Spray a baking dish with cooking spray. Put the sausage mixture on the bottom of the baking dish. Top with cheese.
3. Pour the beaten eggs over the cheese and sausage. Sprinkle garlic salt over the eggs.
4. Put the trivet in the low position in the ninja, and then put the baking dish on top.
5. Set to Air Crisp for 15 minutes at 200C.
6. Carefully remove and serve.

Per Serving: 300kcal
Fat: 20g, Carbohydrates: 3g, Protein: 15g

Serving Size **2 Servings**

Total Time **50 Minutes**

BAKED POTATO

Ingredients

- 2 (227g each) Russet potatoes
- 2 tsp oil
- Salt & pepper to taste
- <u>Optional Toppings</u>
- sour cream
- butter
- green onions or chives
- cheese

Directions

1. Poke holes with a fork on both sides of the potato. Brush the potato skin with oil. Roll each potato on salt.
2. Place the potatoes in the crisping basket and air crisp function at 230C for 45 mins.
3. When time up, remove the potatoes from the basket, cut a slit or two in the top.
4. Top with all your favorite toppings and enjoy!

Per Serving: 219kcal
Fat: 5g, Carbohydrates: 40g, Protein: 8g

Serving Size
6 Servings

Total Time
30 Minutes

JOJO POTATO WEDGES

Ingredients

- **4 large russet potatoes, (scrubbed, cut into wedges & soaked in cold water for 30 mins**
- **100g flour**
- **1 tsp. garlic powder**
- **1 tsp. onion powder**
- **1 tsp. smoked paprika**
- **Pinch of cayenne**
- **2 large egg**
- **2 tbsp. water**
- **Salt & pepper to taste**
- **Cooking spray**

Directions

1. In a large mixing bowl, add flour, garlic powder, onion powder, paprika, cayenne and season with salt & pepper. Mix until combined.
2. In a medium mixing bowl, whisk eggs and water.
3. Pat the potato dry, then dredge them in the flour mixture, then dredge them into the egg then back into the flour.
4. Put wedges in the ninja basket in a single layer. Spray the wedges with cooking spray.
5. Air crisp at 205°C for 18 minutes flipping & spraying them with cooking spray halfway through cooking time.
6. When time is up, remove from ninja, and serve with favorite dipping sauce.

calories: 290kcal, carbohydrates: 50g, protein: 8g, fat: 4g, fiber: 5g, sugar: 2g

Serving Size
8 Servings

Total Time
35 Minutes

MASHED POTATOES

Ingredients

- 1.5 kg Russet potatoes, (peeled & cut into cubes)
- 800ml water
- 3 tsp salt
- 180ml heavy cream, (warm)
- 60g butter, (melted)

Directions

1. Add all ingredients (except butter & cream) to the inner pot of the foodi.
2. Secure lid with valve in seal position. Cook on High pressure for 5 minutes. When time is up, let it naturally release for 5 minutes then do a quick release.
3. Open the lid, take the potatoes and put it in a bowl. Drain the water out of the inner pot and put the potatoes back to the pot.
4. Turn foodi to sear/sauté to medium and sauté for just 5 minutes until the potatoes are dry.
5. Transfer the potatoes to a large mixing bowl. Add in ¼ of cream and butter mixture and either use a hand mixer on low to ncorporate into the potatoes. don't over mix. Continue to add butter and cream until you reach the desired consistency. Season with salt. Serve.

Per (1/3 cup) Serving: 47kcal
Fat: 8g, Carbohydrates: 32g, Protein:4g

Serving Size
3 Servings

Total Time
15 Minutes

CHEESY GARLIC BREAD

Ingredients

- 3 slices French or Italian Bread
- 2 tbsp softened butter
- 1/2 tsp garlic powder
- 120G mozzarella cheese

Directions

1. Butter bread slices and sprinkle with garlic powder.
2. Put bread on lowest inside the ninja pot. Sprinkle cheese on top.
3. Air crisp at 180C for 8 minute.

Per Serving: 310kcal
Fat: 13g, Carbohydrates: 37g, Protein: 12g

Serving Size
10 Servings

Total Time
15 Minutes

MUSHROOM PIES

Ingredients

- 2 tbsp oil
- 1 onion, (chopped)
- 1 garlic clove, (minced)
- 200g mushrooms, (sliced)
- 1/2 tsp chilli flakes
- 1/2 tsp dried thyme
- 2 tbsp double cream
- 320g puff pastry, (thawed)
- 1 egg, (beaten)
- Cooking spray
- Salt & Pepper to taste

Directions

1. Turn the ninja in "Sauté" mode. Add the oil. When the oil is hot, add the onion and garlic, sauté for 2 mins.
2. Add the mushrooms, thyme, chilli powder, and season with salt & pepper. Cook for 5 mins. Then add the cream. Let it cool.
3. Cut the puff pastry into squares and then cut each square into a rectangular strip.
4. Spread the cooled mushroom mixture on the rolled-out pastry leaving 1cm on edges.
5. Brush with beaten egg around the edges of the pastry, then fold the pastry in half over the filling to form a square. Repeat.
6. Grease Ninja foodi pot/basket with cooking spray and put the pastries.
7. Air Crisp for 10 mins at 170 C. Flipping halfway through cooking time.

Per Serving: 226kcal
Fat: 17g, Carbohydrates: 17g, Protein: 4g

Serving Size
6 Servings

Total Time
18 Minutes

COURGETTE FRIES

Ingredients

- *2 medium courgette, (cut into fries)*
- *180g plain flour*
- *2 eggs, (beaten)*
- *250g breadcrumbs*
- *60g grated Parmesan cheese*
- *Salt & pepper to taste*

Directions

1. In a medium mixing bowl, add flour. In another mixing bowl, add beaten eggs. In a 3rd bowl, mix breadcrumbs, cheese and season with salt & pepper.
2. Dip each courgettei fries in the flour, shake off the excess. Then coat with eggs. Finally coat it with breadcrumb mixture.
3. Put it in a greased Ninja foodi pot/basket. Coat them again with cooking spray. (you may need to work in batches)
4. Air crisp at 200C for 8 mins or until browned.

Per Serving: 230kcal
Fat: 5g, Carbohydrates:20g, Protein:10g

Serving Size
3 Servings

Total Time
25 Minutes

CAJUN SEASONED SWEET POTATO

Ingredients

- **350g sweet potato, cut into 1/2cm fries**
- **1 tbsp olive oil**
- **½ tbsp sugar**
- **1 tsp smoked paprika**
- **½ tsp salt**
- **½ tsp garlic powder**
- **½ tsp onion powder**
- **½ tsp dried oregano**
- **½ tsp red pepper flakes**
- **¼ tsp black pepper**
- **¼ tsp ground thyme**

Directions

1. In a large bowl, add fries, olive oil and toss to coat.
2. Put the sweet potato fries in the foodi basket and air crisp for 18 mins at 205C.
3. In a mixing bowl, mix the remaining seasoning ingredients together while the fries cook.
4. Once done, transfer the fries back to the bowl and toss with the spices. Return to the basket and air fry for an additional 6 minutes.

Per Serving: 220kcal
Fat: 7g, Carbohydrates: 38g, Protein: 3g

Serving Size 4 Servings **Total Time** 25 Minutes

SWEET POTATO FRIES

Ingredients

- *3 sweet potatoes, (peeled & cut into fries)*
- *2 tbsp. olive oil*
- *1/4 tsp. black pepper*
- *1/4 tsp. smoked paprika*
- *1/2 tsp garlic powder*
- *Salt to taste*
- *Cooking spray*

Directions

1. Turn the Ninja foodi to 200C and preheat it for 5 minutes. Spray the basket with cooking spray.
2. Put the sweet potatoes into a bowl, drizzle with oil, Season with salt, pepper, paprika, and garlic powder. Mix to coat.
3. Put sweet potato fries in a single layer into the foodi basket (in batches).
4. Air Crisp at 200C for 15 minutes, flipping them halfway through the cooking time.
5. Continue cooking the remaining batches.
6. Serve immediately with your favorite dipping.

Per Serving: 230kcal
Fat: 8g, Carbohydrates:30g, Protein:3g

Serving Size
6 Servings

Total Time
25 Minutes

GREEN BEAN CASSEROLE

Ingredients

- *350g fresh green beans*
- *225g portobello mushrooms*
- *1 small onion, (chopped)*
- *½ tsp thyme leaves, dried*
- *6 garlic cloves, (minced)*
- *250ml beef/chicken stock*
- *120ml heavy cream*
- *60g butter room temperature*
- *30g flour*
- *80g crispy fried onions*
- *Salt & pepper to taste*

Directions

1. Add green beans, mushrooms, onion, thyme, and garlic to the foodi inner pot, then season with salt & pepper. Add stock. Stir .
2. Put a trivet in the high position in the foodi.
3. In a 16cm pan, add butter and flour and mix to form a paste. Cover the pan and put in on trivet.
4. Secure lid with valve in seal position. Cook on High pressure for 0 minutes. When time is up, do a quick release.
5. Remove the butter/flour pan and the trivet.
6. Mix the butter/flour and add it to the green beans mixture. Add heavy cream and stir.
7. Turn the Foodi in sear/sauté on low and heat until the sauce thickens. Stir and serve topped with crispy fried onions .

Per Serving: 330kcal
Fat: 24g, Carbohydrates: 23g, Protein:5g

19

Serving Size
4 Servings

Total Time
22 Minutes

AIR FRIED VEGETABLES

Ingredients

- *400g potatoes, (peeled & cut into small chunks)*
- *2 carrots, (peeled & cut into small chunks)*
- *1 parsnip, (peeled & cut into small chunks)*
- *1 swede, (peeled & cut into small chunks)*
- *1 red onion, (chopped)*
- *2 tbsp. olive oil*
- *2 tsp. paprika*
- *1½ tsp. garlic powder*
- *½ tsp. dried oregano*
- *Salt & pepper to taste*

Directions

1. Coat the all the vegetables (except onion) in 2 tbsp. oil and select air crisp for 15 minutes at 200C.
2. In a large mixing bowl, mix paprika, dried oregano, garlic, salt & pepper.
3. After 15 min, add the potatoes, carrots, parsnips, swede & onions to the bowl and toss with 1 tbsp oil. Air crisp for an additional 7 minutes.

Per Serving: 420kcal
Fat: 8g, Carbohydrates: 25g, Protein:5g

Serving Size
12 Servings

Total Time
40 Minutes

HONEY BUTTER CORNBREAD

Ingredients

- *125ml half & half milk*
- *1 tbsp. white vinegar*
- *2 large eggs*
- *110g brown sugar*
- *50g white sugar*
- *187g all purpose flour*
- *80g yellow cornmeal*
- *113 grams melted butter*
- *1 tsp. salt*
- *2 tsp. baking powder*
- *230g corn kernels*

<u>Honey Butter</u>

- *3 tbsp. melted butter*
- *2 tbsp. honey*

Directions

1. In a medium mixing bowl, mix the vinegar with the half & half.
2. Turn the Foodi in sear/sauté and let the pot heat up.
3. In a large mixing bowl, whisk eggs and sugar, then add flour and cornmeal and mix together. Add the melted butter, salt, baking powder and the milk mixture, mix until combined. Fold in the corn kernels.
4. Turn the Foodi down to medium heat and spray the bottom and sides of the pot with cooking spray.
5. Pour the batter into the inner pot and let it cook for about 10 mins.
6. Close the crisping lid and select bake/roast at 150°C for 20 mins, until the center is cooked all the way.
7. Remove the pot from the foodi and flip out onto a cooling rack.
8. Combine melted butter and honey, poke holes in the cornbread. Spoon the honey/butter over the cornbread. Cool and Serve.

Per Serving: 268kcal
Fat: 12g, Carbohydrates: 37g, Protein:4g

Serving Size
6 Servings

Total Time
14 Minutes

CAULIFLOWER FRIED RICE

Ingredients

- 2½ tbsp sesame oil
- 1 carrot, (diced into 2cm cubes)
- 1 red bell pepper, (diced into 2cm cubes)
- 2 stalks celery, (diced into 2cm cubes)
- 2 tsp soy sauce
- 1 tbsp lemongrass paste
- 1 tsp grated ginger
- ½ tsp chili garlic sauce
- 2 tbsp honey
- 400g uncooked cauliflower rice
- 80g frozen peas
- 2 large eggs, (beaten)
- 2 tbsp green onion, (diced)

Directions

1. Turn the foodi in "Sauté" mode. Add butter. Once hot, add carrot, celery and sauté on high for 3 minutes, stirring constantly.
2. Add soy sauce, lemongrass, ginger, chili garlic sauce, and honey. Stir. Add cauliflower rice and stir.
3. Close the Tender Crisp lid. Air crisp 190°C and for 15 minutes. Stir halfway through cooking time.
4. Add peas and stir. Turn the foodi in "Sauté" mode. Push the cauliflower rice to the edges of the pot. Add oil to the center and let it heat up for about 3 minutes.
5. Pour eggs to the center of the pot. Allow the eggs to set and then break them apart. Add green onions and stir.

Per (1/2 cup) Serving: 108kcal
Fat: 6g, Carbohydrates: 8g, Protein: 4g

Serving Size
6 Servings

Total Time
20 Minutes

MEXICAN RICE

Ingredients

- 2 tbsp oil
- 200g basmati rice
- 1 onion, (finely chopped)
- 1 small carrot, (finely chopped)
- ½ red bell pepper, (diced)
- 1 jalapeno pepper, (diced)
- 2 tbsp tomato paste
- 500ml water
- 1½ tsp ground cumin
- 1½ tsp smoked paprika
- Salt & pepper to taste

Directions

1. Turn the foodi in "Sauté" mode. Add butter. Once hot, add rice and sauté on high for 5 minutes, stirring constantly.
2. Add in the vegetables and the seasoning. Stir and sauté 5 minutes. Add tomato paste and water. Stir
3. Secure lid with valve in seal position. Select steam for 8 minutes.
4. When time is up, open the lid and stir rice.
5. Serve.

Per (1/2 cup) Serving: 180kcal
Fat: 5g, Carbohydrates: 30g, Protein: 3g

Serving Size
4 Servings

Total Time
15 Minutes

LEMON & PARMESAN ORZO

Ingredients

- *30g butter*
- *1 tbsp olive oil*
- *1 onion, (chopped)*
- *Zest of 1 lemon*
- *250g orzo*
- *625ml chicken/vegetable stock*
- *90g grated Parmesan cheese*
- *2 tbsp. lemon juice*
- *Salt & pepper to taste*

Directions

1. Turn the ninja in "Sauté" mode, heat the butter & oil, then add onion, season with salt & pepper and saute for 3 minutes.
2. Then add lemon zest and orzo.
3. Select Cancel and add stock. Cook on high for 5 minutes. When time is up, do a Quick release.
4. Open the lid, sprinkle over the cheese and lemon juice and mix everything together. Serve hot with your favorite protien.

Per Serving: 407kcal
Fat: 15g, Carbohydrates: 50g, Protein:11g

Serving Size
5 Servings

Total Time
15 Minutes

BUTTERED NOODLES

Ingredients

- 225 dry egg noodles
- 1 liter chicken broth
- 100g Butter
- 1 tbsp dried parsley

Directions

1. Put noodles in the bottom of ninja pot. Add remaining ingredients.
2. Secure lid with valve in seal position. Cook on high for 3 minutes.
3. When time is up, let the pressure release naturally for 5 minutes, then do a quick release.
4. Serve with your favorite protein as a main dish.

Per Serving: 290kcal
Fat: 17g, Carbohydrates: 28g, Protein: 6g

Serving Size
8 Servings

Total Time
18 Minutes

MAC & CHEESE

Ingredients

- **2 tbsp salted melted butter**
- **2 tbsp flour**
- **170g evaporated milk**
- **500ml water**
- **230g elbow macaroni**
- **113g yellow cheddar cheese**
- **113g grated white cheddar cheese**

Directions

1. In a pan, mix butter and flour. Stir until a smooth paste is formed. Add evaporated milk and stir. Cover the pan with foil.
2. Add water to the inner pot of foodi. Add in macaroni and stir.
3. Place the trivet on top of the macaroni in the high position. Put the pan with the butter/flour mixture on top.
4. Secure lid with valve in seal position. Cook on High pressure for 3 minutes. When time is up, let it naturally release for 2 minutes then do a quick release.
5. Open the lid, remove the pan and the trivet. mix the butter/flour mixture and pour into macaroni and stir. Add cheese and stir until melted.
6. Serve.

Per Serving: 282kcal
Fat: 14g, Carbohydrates: 25g, Protein: 11g

Serving Size
2 Servings

Total Time
15 Minutes

PENNE POMODORO

Ingredients

- *2 tbsp. olive oil*
- *4 garlic cloves, (minced)*
- *1 onion, (chopped)*
- *1/2 tsp chilli flakes*
- *275ml water*
- *225g penne pasta*
- *400g tinned pureed tomatoes*
- *1 tbsp. tomato puree*
- *1 tbsp. butter*
- *3 tbsp grated Parmesan cheese*
- *Salt & pepper to taste*

Directions

1. Turn the ninja in "Sauté" mode, heat the oil, then add onion and garlic and saute for 5 minutes.
2. Add chilli, water, penne, tomato, tomato puree, and season with salt & pepper.
3. Secure lid with valve in seal position
4. Cook on manual high pressure for 5 minutes.
5. When time is up, do a Quick release.
6. Open the lid and mix everything together, stir in butter and sprinkle with Parmesan Serve.

Per Serving: 350kcal
Fat: 26g, Carbohydrates: 21g, Protein:13g

Serving Size
4 Servings

Total Time
20 Minutes

CREAMY RIGATONI

Ingredients

- *500g rigatoni*
- *2 tbsp. olive oil*
- *110g breadcrumbs*
- *1/2 tsp red pepper flakes*
- *225g ricotta cheese*
- *30g grated Parmesan cheese, grated*

Directions

1. Add Rigatoni to inner pot and pour over 1 liter water to cover Pasta.
2. Secure lid with valve in seal position. Cook on high for 6 minutes. When time is up, let the pressure release naturally. Strain, reserving 3 tbsp. pasta water.
3. Put pasta back to the pot with 3 tbsp. pasta water.
4. Add the Ricotta & Parmesan to the pasta and stir. Then sprinkle Parmesan on top.

Per Serving: 500kcal
Fat: 30g, Carbohydrates: 35g, Protein: 11g

Serving Size
6 Servings

Total Time
14 Minutes

LEMON GARLIC PASTA WITH VEGETABLES

Ingredients

- *2 bell peppers, (diced)*
- *300g cherry tomatoes, (halved)*
- *1 lemon juice and zest*
- *6 garlic cloves, (minced)*
- *1 onion, (diced)*
- *300g dry pasta*
- *120g fresh spinach*
- *500ml vegetable stock*
- *4 tbsp salted butter*
- *30g grated Parmesan cheese*
- *Salt & pepper to taste*

Directions

1. Put onions, garlic, and peppers in the foodi inner pot. Break the pasta in half and put it in the pot.
2. Pour stock over the pasta and add the lemon juice.
3. Secure lid with valve in seal position. Cook on High pressure for zero minutes. When time is up, do a quick release.
4. Open the lid, add tomatoes, lemon zest, and spinach. Mix until the spinach starts to wilt. Season with salt & pepper, add butter and cheese. Stir until cheese melts.
5. Top with some grated parmesan cheese and serve.

Per Serving: 280kcal
Fat: 10g, Carbohydrates: 40g, Protein: 9g

Serving Size
6 Servings

Total Time
14 Minutes

2

Beef & Poultry Mains

Serving Size
12 Servings

Total Time
35 Minutes

CHICKEN FAJITAS

Ingredients

- *900g chicken thighs, (boneless, skinless and cut into bite size slices)*
- *1 red bell pepper, (chopped)*
- *1 green bell pepper, (chopped)*
- *1 onion, (chopped)*
- *2 tbsp. fajita or taco seasoning*
- *Cooking spray*
- *Salt & pepper to taste*
- *Corn/flour tortillas*

Directions

1. Spray the ninja basket with cooking spray.
2. Add the chicken, peppers, onion, and seasoning to the basket. Mix it together. Then spray evenly with cooking spray.
3. Air Crisp at 200C for 20 minutes. stirring & spraying with another coat of cooking spray halfway through the cooking time.
4. Serve with warm tortillas.

Per Serving: 170kcal
Fat: 8g, Carbohydrates: 6g, Protein:19g

Serving Size
4 Servings

Total Time
23 Minutes

CHICKEN TERIYAKI RICE

Ingredients

- **450g chicken breast (Boneless, skinless & cut into 2.5cm pieces)**
- **300g white rice**
- *400ml chicken stock*
- 160ml teriyaki sauce
- 1 tbsp soy sauce
- *225g white mushrooms, (sliced)*
- 1 tbsp oil
- **Salt & pepper to taste**

Directions

1. Turn the foodi in "Sauté" mode. Add oil. Once hot, add chicken, season with salt & pepper and sauté until browned on all sides.
2. Add in all ingredients (except teriyaki and soy sauce). Stir.
3. Secure lid with valve in seal position. Cook on High pressure for 3 minutes. When time is up, let it naturally release for 10 minutes then do a quick release.
4. Open the lid and add teriyaki and soy sauce, stir rice. Serve.

Per Serving: 216kcal
Fat: 6g, Carbohydrates: 11g, Protein: 28g

Serving Size
8 Servings

Total Time
25 Minutes

BUTTER CHICKEN

Ingredients

- 2 tsp oil
- 6 garlic cloves, minced
- 1 tbsp grated fresh ginger
- 60g tomato paste
- 225g tomato puree
- 1 tbsp garam masala
- 2 tsp turmeric
- ½ tsp cumin
- 1 cinnamon stick (or 1/4 tsp. ground cinnamon)
- 225ml chicken stock
- 900g boneless, skinless chicken breasts

For the rice

- 200g long grain or jasmine rice, rinsed & drained
- 225ml chicken stock
- 60g butter
- 125ml double cream
- Salt & pepper to taste

Directions

1. Turn the ninja in "Sauté" mode. Add the oil. When the oil is hot, add the garlic and ginger and cook, stirring, until fragrant, about 1 minute. Add the tomato paste, tomato puree, garam masala, turmeric, salt and cumin and cook for 3 minutes, stirring occasionally.
2. Turn off the sauté function and add the cinnamon stick, chicken stock and stir together. Put the chicken breasts inside.
3. Put the trivet over the chicken and place a 7cm baking bowl on top. Add the rice and water to the bowl.
4. Secure lid with valve in seal position. Cook on high pressure for 17 minutes. When time is up, do a quick release.
5. Open the lid, Remove the rice and the trivet. Ruffle the rice and set aside. Remove chicken and dice into bite-size pieces.
6. Press the sauté button and add butter and cream and cook until they thicken slightly, about 2 minutes.
7. Add the diced chicken to the Ninja Foodi to heat.
8. Serve the chicken with the rice and garnish with cilantro, if desired.

Per Serving: 415kcal
Fat: 18g, Carbohydrates: 24g, Protein: 38g

Serving Size
6 Servings

Total Time
35 Minutes

CHICKEN STIR FRY

Ingredients

- 900g Boneless, Skinless Chicken Thighs (Cut into Chunks)
- 350g Bag of Frozen Stir Fry Vegetables
- Cooking Spray

<u>Sauce</u>
- 85g Honey
- 100ml Soy Sauce
- 2 Tbsp Brown Sugar
- 2 Tbsp Ketchup
- 1 Clove Crushed Garlic
- 1/2 Tsp Ground Ginger
- 1 Tbsp Cornstarch

Directions

1. Coat the chicken with cooking spray, place it into the basket of the Ninja. Air Crisp at 200C for 20-25 minutes.
2. Once cooked, add in the frozen vegetables on top of the chicken. Air crisp for an additional 5 mins.
3. Once done, remove the chicken and vegetables and set them aside.
4. Turn the ninja in "Sauté" mode. Add honey, soy sauce, brown sugar, ketchup, garlic, and ginger. mix until combine and bring to a boil. Add cornstarch and stir until thicken.
5. Add in the chicken and vegetables to the sauce and coat well.
6. Serve over noodles.

Per Serving: 440kcal
Fat: 15g, Carbohydrates: 35g, Protein: 35g

Serving Size: 3 Servings

Total Time: 15 Minutes

GREEK CHICKEN WRAP

Ingredients

For the Veggies

- *200g red onion, (diced)*
- *250g bell pepper, (diced)*
- *340g grape tomatoes*
- *1 tbsp. olive oil*
- *1 tsp garlic Powder*
- *1 tsp onion powder*
- *1/2 tsp dried oregano*

For the Greek Chicken

- *450g boneless & skinless chicken breast, (diced)*
- *1 tbsp. olive oil*
- *1 tbsp. Greek seasoning*
- *Salt & pepper to taste*

Directions

1. In a large bowl, add bell pepper and tomatoes. Toss with the 1 Tbsp of olive oil and spices before placing in the ninja basket. Air crisp for 10 mins at 205C.
2. In the same bowl, add the chicken, remaining olive oil, Greek seasoning, salt & black pepper. Mix to coat the chicken.
3. After the veggies have cooked for 10 mins, transfer to a clean bowl. Set aside.
4. Add the chicken to the foodi basket and cook for 8 mins. After the chicken is cooked, add the veggies back to the basket and use the Foodi's broil for 8 mins.
5. Remove, serve in wraps with lettuce.

Per Serving: 250kcal
Fat: 6g, Carbohydrates: 9g, Protein: 22g

Serving Size
5 Servings

Total Time
15 Minutes

BBQ CHICKEN LEGS

Ingredients

- **6 chicken drumsticks**
- *Garlic salt to taste*
- **Barbecue Sauce to taste**

Directions

1. Season the chicken legs with garlic salt and place in ninja basket. Air crisp at 180C for 15 minutes.
2. Once done brush with BBQ sauce and flip and top with BBQ sauce. Air fry at for another 15 mins.
3. Remove from ninja and brush with additional BBQ sauce before serving.

Per Serving: 120kcal
Fat: 7g, Carbohydrates: 1g, Protein:13g

Serving Size
4 Servings

Total Time
25 Minutes

SWEET & SOUR CHICKEN

Ingredients

Chicken

- **1 kg boneless skinless chicken breasts, cut into cubes**
- **salt and pepper to taste**
- **125g cornstarch 1 scant cup**

Sweet & Sour Sauce

- **100g granulated sugar**
- **120g ketchup**
- **240g apple cider vinegar**
- **2 tbsp soy sauce**
- **2 tsp garlic salt**

Directions

1. Add the chicken to a Ziploc bag with cornstarch, salt, and pepper. Shake to coat evenly.
2. Spray ninja basket with cooking spray.
3. Remove chicken from the bag and shake off any excess coating. Add chicken in a single layer in ninja basket and spray tops with cooking spray.
4. Air crisp at 205°C for 10 minutes. Flip at halfway point.
5. Whisk sauce ingredients together in oven safe dish. Add in the chicken and cook for 5 minutes. Chicken will register at 165°F/74°C with an instant read thermometer once it is finished cooking.

Calories: 589kcal | Carbohydrates: 63g | Protein: 61g | Fat: 7g | Sodium: 2058mg | Fiber: 1g | Sugar: 32g

Serving Size 6 Servings

Total Time 80 Minutes

CRISPED WHOLE CHICKEN

Ingredients

- **2250g chicken thawed**
- **1 tbsp. olive oil**

<u>Seasoning Blend</u>

- **1 tsp. salt**
- **½ tsp. black pepper**
- **½ tsp. onion powder**
- **½ tsp. garlic powder**
- **¼ tsp. dried thyme leaves**

Directions

1. Pat chicken dry with paper towels and coat the chicken with oil. Sprinkle the seasoning blend on the chicken first and then place it on the foodi rack.
2. Add 250ml of chicken broth to the inner pot and place the rack with the chicken into the inner pot.
3. Secure lid with valve in seal position. Select the steam function and set the time for 6 minutes. When the time is up, select the air crisp at 90°C for 60 minutes.
4. When time is up, allow the chicken to rest for a full 10 minutes before serving.

Per Serving: 275kcal
Fat: 15g, Carbohydrates: 12g, Protein: 20g

Serving Size
6 Servings

Total Time
22 Minutes

CHICKEN POT PIE

Ingredients

Pie Crust
- 300g plain flour
- 1 tsp salt
- 270g unsalted butter, (cut into small cubes)
- 5 to 6 tbsp iced water

Pie Filling
- 75g plus 1 tbsp unsalted butter, divided
- 1 onion, (diced)
- 1 celery stalk, (chopped)
- 125ml chicken stock
- 2 large boneless skinless chicken breasts, (cut into bite-size pieces)
- large potatoes, (cut into 2.5cm cubes)
- 1/4 tsp dried thyme
- 140g frozen peas and carrots
- 50g plain flour
- 125ml milk, plus more as needed
- Cooking spray
- Salt & pepper to taste

Per Serving: 800kcal
Fat: 43g, Carbohydrates: 60g, Protein: 25g

Directions

1. In a large mixing bowl, add flour & salt. Mix until combined. Add the butter into the flour mixture, Mash with a fork until it resembles a very coarse meal. Gradually add water until the dough just sticks together into a ball.
2. Turn the Ninja Foodi on the sauté mode and add the 1 tbsp butter. Add onion, celery and sauté for 3 minutes, until tender. Add chicken stock, chicken, potatoes, thyme, and season with salt & pepper.
3. Secure lid with valve in seal position. Cook on High for 3 minutes. When time is up, do a quick release.
4. Open the lid. Add the peas and carrots.
5. In a small saucepan over medium heat, add remaining butter. Whisk in the flour. Cook for 3 minutes, until bubbly. Gradually add milk, stirring for 2 more minutes, until the sauce is thick and creamy. Remove from heat, add into the chicken mixture to combine well. Add more milk, if needed.
6. Spray a deep-dish pie with cooking spray.
7. Transfer the pie crust into floured surface and roll it into a circle that's at least 2.5cm larger than the baking dish.
8. Pour chicken mixture into the pie dish. Top with the pie crust (poke some holes in the crust top). Bake for 10 minutes at 220C. Remove from Ninja and let cool for 5 minutes before serving.

Serving Size
6 Servings

Total Time
25 Minutes

CORNISH HENS

Ingredients

- 2 (450-700g) Cornish hens, (thawed)
- ½ tsp. dried rosemary
- ½ tsp. lemon zest
- ¼ tsp. dried thyme
- ¼ tsp. garlic powder
- Salt & pepper to taste
- Cooking spray

Directions

1. Pat the Cornish hens dry and rub the seasoning over them evenly.
2. Put them breast side down in the basket of the ninja. Coat the hens with cooking spray and air crisp for 20 mins at 185C.
3. Flip the hens and cook for an additional 20 mins.
4. Remove and let rest for 10 mins then cut and serve.

Per Serving: 100kcal
Fat: 7g, Carbohydrates: 1g, Protein:15g

Serving Size
3 Servings

Total Time
14 Minutes

CHICKEN SOUVLAKI

Ingredients

- *1 chicken breast, (cut into 2.5cm chunks)*
- *Juice & zest of a small lemon*
- *3 garlic cloves, (minced)*
- *1 tsp. olive oil*
- *1 tsp. Greek yogurt*
- *1 tbsp. dried oregano*
- *1/2 tsp. dried thyme*
- *Salt & pepper to taste*

Directions

1. In a large mixing bowl, add chicken, garlic, lemon juice & zest, oregano, thyme, season with salt & pepper. Mix until all combined. Set aside in refrigerator for at least 30 minutes.
2. After 30 minutes, take chicken out of refrigerator, add Greek yogurt, and oil. Mix to coat the chicken.
3. Put the chicken onto skewers, then put in foodi and air crisp at 180C for 9 minutes, flipping half way through cooking time.
4. Remove, serve.

Per Serving: 80kcal
Fat: 3g, Carbohydrates: 8g, Protein: 12g

Serving Size: 2 Servings
Total Time: 35 Minutes

CHICKEN DRUMSTICKS

Ingredients

- **6 chicken Legs**
- **1/2 tsp smoked paprika**
- **1 tsp garlic powder**
- **1 tsp onion powder**
- **1 tbsp baking powder**
- **Salt & pepper to taste**

Directions

1. Pat dry chicken legs.
2. In a large mixing bowl, mix salt, black pepper, paprika, garlic powder, onion powder and baking powder.
3. Sprinkle the seasoning mixture on the chicken legs and toss to coat
4. Place the chicken on the foodi basket. Drizzle with oil.
5. Air Crisp on 200C for 15 mins per side.

Per Serving: 280kcal
Fat: 18g, Carbohydrates: 4g, Protein: 21g

Serving Size
6 Servings

Total Time
20 Minutes

STUFFED CHICKEN BREASTS

Ingredients

- 2 medium sized chicken breasts
- 120g Provolone Cheese slices
- 80g Beef Bresaola
- 120 Salami
- 1 large egg, (beaten)
- 100g bread crumbs
- 1 tsp Italian Seasoning
- 1 tbsp butter, (melted)
- Cooking spray
- Salt & pepper to taste

Directions

1. Cut chicken breasts in half horizontally through the middle. With meat tenderizer pound the chicken breasts to about 1/2cm thin. Season with salt & pepper.
2. Put 3 provolone slices, 3 salami slices, and 2 Bresaola slices on each chicken breast. Roll the chicken breast and secure with, toothpicks.
3. Preheat the foodi with the basket in on Air Crisp at 200°C for 10 minutes.
4. In a shallow dish, mix bread crumbs and Italian seasoning.
5. Roll the chicken in the beaten egg and then coat with breadcrumbs.
6. Spray foodi basket with cooking spray. Put chicken breasts in the basket, brush with butter.
7. Close the lid. Air Crisp for 10 minutes. Flip, brush with butter and cook another 10 minutes.
8. Remove from the basket and let cool for 5 minutes. Serve.

Per Serving: 450kcal
Fat: 20g, Carbohydrates: 16g, Protein:30g

Serving Size
4 Servings

Total Time
40 Minutes

ONION CHICKEN

Ingredients

- 2 tbsp olive oil
- 2 tbsp salted butter
- 2 large chicken breasts, (cut in half through the middle)
- 640g onions, (sliced into thin slices)
- 1 tbsp cornstarch
- 300ml beef stock
- 4 slices Swiss cheese
- 1 tsp dried thyme
- Salt & pepper to taste

Directions

1. Season chicken with thyme, salt & pepper.
2. Turn the foodi in "Sauté" mode. Add butter. Once hot, place the chicken breasts into the inner pot and sear for 4 minutes. Flip and add onions. Sear the chicken for another 4 minutes.
3. Remove the chicken and transfer them to a plate. Season the onion with thyme, salt & pepper.
4. Close Tender crisp lid and select broil for 10 minutes.
5. In a small mixing bowl, mix cornstarch with 2 tbsp of beef stock and stir to combine.
6. When time is up, open the lid and turn the sear/sauté on high and deglaze with the remaining beef stock, scrape the bottom to release any browned bits.
7. Add the cornstarch mixture and stir. Add chicken back to the pot and bring to a boil for 3 minutes. Reduce heat and simmer for 5 minutes.
8. Cover each chicken piece with Swiss cheese. Broil for 5 minutes until the cheese is melted.

Per Serving: 450kcal
Fat: 18g, Carbohydrates: 20g, Protein: 30g

Serving Size
10 Servings

Total Time
25 Minutes

AHEAD SHREDDED CHICKEN

Ingredients

- *2250g frozen bone-in chicken thighs*
- *1 stick butter*
- *250ml chicken broth*
- *Salt & pepper to taste*
- *Garlic powder to taste*

Directions

1. Put all ingredients in the bottom of foodi pot.
2. Secure lid with valve in seal position. Cook on high pressure for 30 minutes.
3. When time is up, do a quick release.
4. Open the lid, transfer chicken into a bowl to remove skin and chicken bone. Shred chicken.
5. Store in an air tight container with a little broth spooned over the top to use in sandwiches, salads, casseroles and soups.
6. Reserve remaining broth as a broth base for soups if desired.

Per Serving: 200kcal
Fat: 25g, Carbohydrates: 1g, Protein: 25g

Serving Size
6 Servings

Total Time
12 Minutes

CHICKEN PAD THAI

Ingredients

- 2 tbsp. olive oil
- 2 chicken breasts, (cut into cubes)
- 3 garlic cloves, (minced)
- 3 tbsp. tamari or soy sauce
- 120g pad thai sauce
- 40g ketchup
- 350ml water
- 200g dry rice noodles
- 2 green onions, (sliced)

Directions

1. Add oil, chicken, garlic, soy sauce, pad Thai sauce, ketchup and rice noodles to the bottom of ninja. Add water until the line is slightly above the noodles.
2. Secure lid with valve in seal position. Cook on high pressure for 2 minutes. When the time is up, do a quick release.
3. Open the lid, let sit for 2 minutes, and then stir.
4. Transfer to a bowl, garnish with green onion and serve.

Per Serving: 380kcal
Fat: 5g, Carbohydrates: 62g, Protein: 19g

Serving Size
6 Servings

Total Time
8 Hours 10 Minutes

CHICKEN CHILI

Ingredients

- *280g cooked chicken, (cut into bite size)*
- *2 400g tins butter beans*
- *400ml chicken broth*
- *400g tin diced tomatoes with green chilies*
- *1 onion, (chopped)*
- *1 tsp. chili powder*
- *1 tsp. ground cumin*
- *3 tbsp. flour*

Directions

1. Put all ingredients (except flour) in the pot of the ninja.
2. Secure lid with valve in seal position. Turn the slow cooker function to low for 8 hours.
3. When time is up, open the lid and add the flour.
4. Secure lid with valve in seal position and cook for another 30 minutes to thicken.
5. Serve.

Per Serving: 300kcal
Fat: 4g, Carbohydrates: 35g, Protein: 22g

Serving Size
6 Servings

Total Time
20 Minutes

CHICKEN ALFREDO

Ingredients

- *1 medium onion, (chopped)*
- *6 cloves garlic, (minced)*
- *1 small yellow bell pepper, (sliced into thin strips)*
- *1 small green bell pepper, (sliced into thin strips)*
- *227g fettuccine*
- *250g chicken breast, (cut into 2cm cubes)*
- *4 Tbsp salted butter*
- *500ml chicken stock*
- *112g Italian blend shredded cheese*
- *50g grated Parmesan cheese*
- *120ml heavy cream*
- *Salt & pepper to taste*

Directions

1. Season chicken with salt & pepper.
2. Add the onions, peppers, garlic to the inner pot. Cut the fettuccine in half and put them on top of the onions. Place the chicken on top. Place the butter on top of the chicken. Pour in the chicken stock.
3. Secure lid with valve in seal position. Cook for 2 minutes. When the time is up, do a quick release.
4. Open the lid, turn the sear/sauté on high. Stir.
5. Add the cheese and stir until combined. Reduce the heat to medium and add cream. Mix until combinedl and serve!

Per Serving: 280kcal
Fat: 20g, Carbohydrates: 37g, Protein: 26g

Serving Size
10 Servings

Total Time
35 Minutes

PICADILLO

Ingredients

- *900g ground beef (96/4)*
- *2 tbsp. olive oil*
- *250g yellow onion, (chopped)*
- *150g green bell pepper, (chopped)*
- *4 garlic cloves, (minced)*
- *240ml beef stock*
- *225g tin tomato sauce*
- *200g tin tomato paste*
- *60ml white grape juice*
- *10 jalapeño stuffed olives, (sliced)*
- *60g raisins*
- *1/2 tbsp. ground cumin*
- *1 tsp. dried oregano*
- *Salt & pepper to taste*

Directions

1. Turn the foodi in "Sauté" mode. Add oil. Once hot, add onion and bell pepper. Cook about 8 minutes. Add garlic and cook until fragrant. Add the ground beef and cook until no pink remains.
2. Add the broth, tomato sauce, tomato paste, grape juice, olives, raisins, cumin, oregano and season with salt & pepper. Stir well.
3. Secure lid with valve in seal position. Cook on high pressure for 8 minutes. When time is up, do a quick release.

Per Serving: 200kcal
Fat: 7.3g, Carbohydrates: 13g, Protein: 21.3g

Serving Size
6 Servings

Total Time
35 Minutes

SOUTHWESTERN CHILI

Ingredients

- *1 tbsp. olive oil*
- *1 onion, (chopped)*
- *450g lean ground beef (80/20)*
- *400g tinned black beans, (rinsed & drained)*
- *280g tin diced tomatoes with chilies*
- *170g tinned corn, (drained)*
- *250ml chicken stock*
- *1/4 tsp. chili powder*
- *1 tsp. smoked paprika*
- *1 tbsp. ground cumin*
- *1 tsp. dried oregano*
- *Salt & pepper to taste*

Directions

1. Turn the ninja in "Sauté" mode, heat the oil, then add the onions and saute for 4 minutes.
2. Add ground beef, and saute until fully cooked. Add all the remaining ingredients, and mix well.
3. Secure lid with valve in seal position. Cook on high pressure for 17 minutes. When the time is up, let the pressure release naturally.
4. Open the lid, stir, and serve.

Per Serving: 385kcal
Fat: 5g, Carbohydrates: 31g, Protein:23g

Serving Size
6 Servings

Total Time
40 Minutes

BEEF STEW

Ingredients

- *900g Beef stew meat*
- *1 Onion, (chopped)*
- *700ml Beef Broth*
- *1 Bay Leaf*
- *2 Tsp Paprika*
- *2 garlic cloves, (minced)*
- *2 Tsp Worcestershire Sauce*
- *3 Russet Potatoes, (peeled & chopped)*
- *2 Carrots, (peeled & chopped)*
- *2 Celery Stalks, (chopped)*
- *1 Beef Bouillon Cube*
- *2 Tbsp Cornstarch*

Directions

1. Turn the ninja in "Sauté" mode. Add the oil. When the oil is hot, add onion and meat and saute until the meat is browned.
2. Add broth, bay leaf, paprika, garlic, Worcestershire sauce, potatoes, carrots, celery, and the bouillon cube.
3. Secure lid with valve in seal position. Cook on high pressure for 30 minutes.
4. When time is up, let the pressure release naturally for 5 minutes, then do a quick release.
5. Open the lid, whisk in the cornstarch to thicken. Let cool for 5 minutes and serve.

Per Serving: 240kcal
Fat: 11g, Carbohydrates: 11g, Protein: 3g

Serving Size
6 Servings

Total Time
1 Hour 30 Minutes

BEEF ROAST

Ingredients

- 1400g beef chuck roast
- 1 tsp. steak seasoning
- 1 package brown gravy mix
- 125ml water
- 4 tbsp. butter
- Parsley or Rosemary to Garnish

Directions

1. Preheat the ninja air crisp at 200C for 5 minutes. Season the roast with steak seasoning.
2. Mix the gravy with water and set aside.
3. Carefully spray the basket of the ninja with cooking spray. Put the roast into the basket and air crisp for 15 mins.
4. Once the cooking time is up, remove the roast and place it on sheet pan lined with foil. Roll up the foil around the sides of the roast and put it back to the basket of ninja. pour the gravy over the roast. Put the butter on top of the roast.
5. Air crisp for 40 minutes at 160C.
6. Once cooked, let it rest for 5 mins, then slice and serve.

Per Serving: 500kcal
Fat: 18g, Carbohydrates: 3g, Protein: 40g

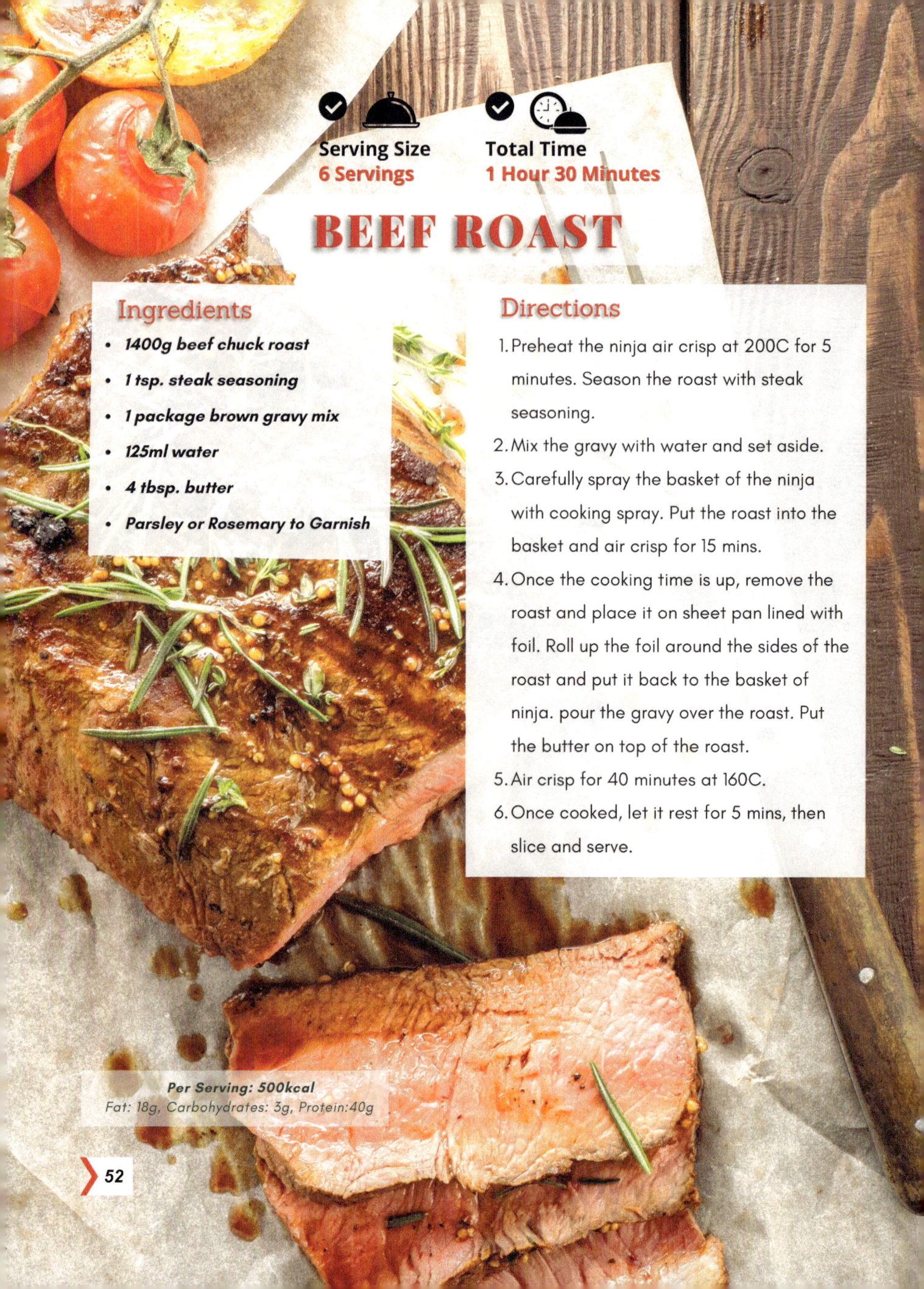

Serving Size
5 Servings

Total Time
55 Minutes

MEATLOAF

Ingredients

- *700g baby potatoes*
- *½ onion, (chopped)*
- *2 garlic cloves, (minced)*
- *170ml chicken broth*

For the meatloaf

- *1 onion, (finely chopped)*
- *1 tbsp. butter*
- *900g lean ground beef*
- *90g seasoned breadcrumbs*
- *80ml milk*
- *1 tbsp. Worcestershire sauce*
- *½ tsp. garlic powder*
- *2 eggs*
- *Salt & pepper to taste*

Per Serving: 200kcal
Fat: 26g, Carbohydrates: 26g, Protein:35g

Directions

1. Turn the Ninja Foodi in "Sauté" mode. Cook the finely chopped onion (for the meatloaf) in butter until tender, about 5 minutes. set aside and let it cool completely.
2. Put baby potatoes, chopped onion, garlic, and stock in bottom of Ninja Foodi.
3. In a large mixing bowl, mix all of the meatloaf ingredients. Form a loaf and place it on a piece of foil. Fold the edges of the foil to make a "skillet" for the meatloaf.
4. Place the meatloaf on the trivet and add to the Ninja Foodi.
5. Secure lid with valve in seal position. Cook on high pressure for 30 minutes. When time is up, let the pressure naturally release for 10 minutes then do a quick release.
6. Air crisp for 10 minutes at 200C.
7. Open the lid. Remove the meatloaf to a cutting board.
8. Rest 10 minutes before cutting. Serve with potatoes.

Serving Size
4 Servings

Total Time
30 Minutes

BEEF STEW WITH MUSHROOMS

Ingredients

- *2 tbsp. olive oil*
- *700g boneless beef chuck roast, (cubed)*
- *2 cloves garlic, (minced)*
- *2 celery stalks, (sliced)*
- *225g mushrooms, (cut into halves)*
- *750ml water*
- *4 medium carrots, (sliced)*
- *2 russet potatoes, (peeled & cubed)*
- *Salt & pepper to taste*

Directions

1. Turn the Ninja Foodi on the sauté mode and add the oil. Brown the cubed beef (work in patches), adding more oil as needed. Using a slotted spoon, remove browned beef from the pot and transfer it into a plate.
2. Add garlic and celery to the Ninja, and stir, cook for 1-2 minutes. Return the beef to Ninja. Add in mushrooms and water. Season with salt and black pepper.
3. Secure lid with valve in seal position. Cook on high pressure for 17 minutes. When time is up, do Quick release.
4. Open the lid and add carrots, and potatoes to the pot.
5. Secure lid with valve in seal position and cook again on high pressure for 5 minutes. When time is up, do Quick release.
6. Open the lid and adjust seasoning. Serve immediately.

Per Serving: 254kcal
Fat: 11g, Carbohydrates: 30g, Protein: 21g

Serving Size
6 Servings

Total Time
20 Minutes

MEATBALLS

Ingredients

- **450g ground beef**
- **1 ½ tbsp Worcestershire sauce**
- **¾ tsp. basil**
- **¾ tsp. onion powder**
- **¾ tsp. garlic powder**
- **1 large egg**
- **40g bread crumbs**
- **Salt & pepper to taste**

Directions

1. Turn the foodi on Air Crisp at 190°C, and let it preheat.
2. In a large mixing bowl, mix ground beef, seasonings, Worcestershire sauce, egg, and bread crumbs.
3. Form meatballs using 2 Tbsp. of mixture per meatball.
4. Spray the basket with cooking spray and put meatballs in a single layer on the basket. (you may need to work in patches)
5. Air Crisp on 190°C for 5 minutes. Then flip and cook another minutes. Remove and Serve.

Per (3 meatballs) Serving: 232kcal
Fat: 16g, Carbohydrates: 6g, Protein:15g

Serving Size 4 Servings

Total Time 16 Minutes

STEAK BITES

Ingredients

- *900g sirloin steak, (cut into 5cm pieces)*
- *2 tbsp oil*
- *1 tsp. garlic powder*
- *2 tbsp. Worcestershire Sauce*
- *Salt & pepper to taste*

Directions

1. In a large mixing bowl, add steak pieces, add the salt, pepper, garlic powder, oil and Worcestershire sauce. Mix.
2. Cover and refrigerate for at least 30 minutes.
3. Preheat ninja foodi by setting the temperature to 200C for 5 minutes.
4. Coat Ninja foodi basket with cooking spray. Add steak pieces into the hot basket.
5. Air crisp for 3 minutes, then flip and air crisp for another 3 minutes.
6. Remove from ninja foodi, serve.

Per Serving: 480kcal
Fat: 14g, Carbohydrates: 2g, Protein:30g

Serving Size
6 Servings

Total Time
55 Minutes

SWISS STEAK

Ingredients

- 2 tbsp olive oil
- 1½kg (1½cm-thick) round steaks
- 30g plain flour
- 200g fresh mushrooms, (sliced)
- ½ tsp onion powder
- ½ tsp garlic powder
- 60ml beef stock
- 400g tin chopped tomatoes
- 1 tsp smoked paprika
- 1 tbsp Worcestershire sauce
- 1 tbsp apple cider vinegar
- 1 onion, (chopped)
- 2 carrots, (sliced)
- Salt & pepper to taste

Directions

1. In a large mixing bowl, add flour, paprika, onion powder, garlic powder and season with salt & pepper. Mix until combined, then dredge the steak on the flour mixture.
2. Turn the foodi in "Sauté" mode. Add oil. Once hot, add coated round steak (work in batches), and sauté for 3 minutes in each side until browned on all sides.
3. Add beef stock, stir and scrape the bottom to loosen any brown bits. Add all ingredients. Add the steak back in.
4. Secure lid with valve in seal position. Cook on High pressure for 25 minutes. When time is up, let it naturally release for 10 minutes then do a quick release.
5. Open the lid. Turn the foodi in "Sauté" mode to thicken the sauce if desired. Serve.

Per Serving: 570kcal
Fat: 17g, Carbohydrates: 11g, Protein: 48g

Serving Size: 8 Servings
Total Time: 85 Minutes

CORNED BEEF WITH CABBAGE & POTATOES

Ingredients

- 1 ½ kg boneless corned beef brisket
- 500ml vegetable stock
- 1 head cabbage, (cut into 8 wedges)
- 250g potatoes , (cut into wedges)
- 250g carrots, (cut into thick fries)
- 2 tbsp melted butter
- 3 bay leaves
- 1 large onion, (peeled & quartered)
- Salt & pepper to taste

Directions

1. Put corned beef and stock in the Ninja foodi pot. Add seasoning over the brisket after water is added.
2. Secure lid with valve in seal position. Cook on high pressure for 80 minutes. When time is up, do Quick release.
3. Remove corned beef from Ninja pot, Add potatoes, carrots and cabbage to the Ninja foodi pot.
4. Secure lid with valve in seal position. Cook on high pressure for 3 minutes. When time is up, do Quick release.
5. Mix butter, salt & pepper, and drizzle over vegetables. Serve brisket with vegetables.

Per Serving: 415kcal
Fat: 26g, Carbohydrates: 15g, Protein: 27.5g

Serving Size
6 Servings

Total Time
60 Minutes

BEEF POT PIE

Ingredients

Pie Crust
- 300g plain flour
- 1 tsp salt
- 270g unsalted butter, (cut into small cubes)
- 5 to 6 tbsp iced water

Pie Filling
- 700g round steaks, (cut into 1.5cm cubes)
- 2 tsp oil
- 1 onion, (diced)
- 2 garlic cloves, (minced)
- 250ml beef stock
- 125ml whole milk
- 2 tbsp flour
- 140g frozen pea and carrot
- Salt & pepper to taste

Directions

1. In a large mixing bowl, add flour & salt. Mix until combined. Add the butter into the flour mixture, Mash with a fork until it resembles a very coarse meal. Gradually add water until the dough just sticks together into a ball.
2. Turn the Ninja Foodi on the sauté mode, add oil. Add beef cubes, season with salt & pepper, cook until browned (work in batches). Add onion and garlic and sauté 3 minutes. Add beef stock, and stir, scrubbing any stuck pieces in the bottom of pot.
3. Secure lid with valve in seal position. Cook on High for 15 minutes. When time is up, do a quick release.
4. In a medium mixing bowl, mix milk, flour and season with salt.
5. Open the lid. Set to sauté, add in flour and milk mixture, simmer 2 minutes. Stir in frozen peas and carrots. Mix and turn off heat.
6. Transfer the pie crust into floured surface and roll it into a 6 circles that's larger than the each ramekin.
7. Spray a six ramekins with cooking spray, divide beef filling into the six ramekins. Top with the pie crust (poke some holes in the crust top). Bake for 15 minutes at 190C. Remove from Ninja and let cool for 5 minutes before serving.

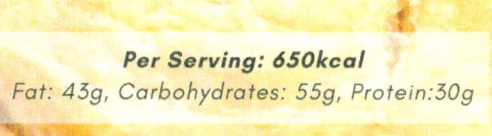

Per Serving: 650kcal
Fat: 43g, Carbohydrates: 55g, Protein:30g

Serving Size
6 Servings

Total Time
20 Minutes

STEAK AND VEGETABLE BOWL

Ingredients

- **2 strip steaks, (cut into strips)**
- **150g red bell pepper, (chopped)**
- **150g green bell pepper, (chopped)**
- **180g yellow squash, (chopped)**
- **100g mushroom, (sliced)**
- **1 onion, (chopped)**
- **1/2 tbsp. steak seasoning**
- **Salt & pepper to taste**
- **Cooking spray**

Directions

1. Spray the Foodi basket with cooking spray.
2. Put the steaks and vegetables in the basket. Sprinkle with the seasoning. Spray with cooking spray.
3. Air Crisp for 7 minutes on 200C.
4. Open the lid. Spray it with cooking spray and mix together. Air Crisp for another 8 minutes.
5. Serve hot.

Per Serving: 140kcal
Fat: 9g, Carbohydrates:7g, Protein:15g

Serving Size
4 Servings

Total Time
40 Minutes

SCOTCH EGG

Ingredients

- *450g minced beef, (90% lean)*
- *5 eggs*
- *1 tsp. dried sage*
- *1/2 tsp red chili flake*
- *1/2 tsp garlic powder*
- *1/2 tsp onion powder*
- *60g plain flour*
- *2 tbsp milk*
- *60g panko bread crumbs*
- *Cooking spray*
- *Salt & pepper to taste*

Directions

1. In medium saucepan over high heat.bring 1 liter of water to a boil; add 4 eggs, boil 5 minutes. Then transfer boiled eggs into a large bowl full with ice water.
2. In a large mixing bowl, add minced beef, all the spices and season with salt & pepper. Mix until all combined.
3. Peel the eggs. Divide the minced beef into 4 portions and form into 1/2cm thick disks. Place the egg in the middle of each disk. Wrap the beef around each egg to fully cover the egg with beef.
4. Prepare three bowls: 1) with flour, 2) egg whisked with milk, and 3) panko. Dredge each egg in flour, dip in egg then roll in panko. Refrigerate Scotch egg for 20 minutes.
5. Set Ninja Foodi to 200°C. Spray each Scotch egg with cooking spray and place in Ninja Foodi. Air crisp for 8 minutes, flip and air crisp for more 7 minutes.

Per Serving: 400kcal
Fat: 13g, Carbohydrates: 20g, Protein:44g

Serving Size
8 Servings

Total Time
45 Minutes

BEEF AND CABBAGE

Ingredients

- *1350g stew beef, (cut into small pieces)*
- *115g butter*
- *250ml beef broth*
- *28g ranch dressing mix*
- *28g Brown Gravy Mix*
- *125ml Pepperoncini Juice*
- *130g sliced pepperoncinis*
- *Small cabbage head, (chopped)*
- *Sesame seeds*
- *Choppeed green onion*

Directions

1. Put all ingredients (except cabbage) in a ninja pot.
2. Secure lid with valve in seal position. Cook on high pressure for 15 minutes.
3. When time is up, do a quick release, open the lid and add cabbage.
4. Secure lid with valve in seal position. Cook on high pressure for 8 minutes.
5. When time is up, do a quick release
6. Sprinkle with Sesame seeds & green onion. serve.

Per Serving: 380kcal
Fat: 18g, Carbohydrates: 5g, Protein: 35g

Serving Size
8 Servings

Total Time
20 Minutes

GROUND BEEF AND RICE

Ingredients

- *450g ground Beef*
- *2 tbsp. chili powder*
- *1/2 tbsp. garlic powder*
- *1/2 tbsp. onion powder*
- *1 tsp. smoked paprika*
- *1/2 tsp ground cumin*
- *1/2 tsp dried oregano*
- *60g Tomato Paste*
- *Juice of 1 large lemon*
- *500ml chicken stock*
- *200g cilantro lime rice (page:)*
- *Salt & pepper to taste*

Directions

1. Turn the foodi in "Sauté" mode. Add the ground beef, add the dry spices. Once the ground beef is fully cooked, add the limon juice and tomato paste, stirring everything together.
2. Add the chicken stock and rice. Stir well.
3. Secure lid with valve in seal position. Cook on high pressure for 5 minutes. When time is up, do a quick release.
4. Open the lid, stir. Serve.

Per Serving: 230kcal
Fat: 8g, Carbohydrates: 18g, Protein:18g

Serving Size
6 Servings

Total Time
60 Minutes

BEEF STROGANOFF

Ingredients

- 1 tbsp olive oil
- 700g beef sirloin, (cut into bites)
- 2 tbsp. unsalted butter
- 1 onion, (chopped)
- 2 garlic cloves, (minced)
- 120g mushrooms, (sliced)
- 800ml beef stock
- 2 tsp Worcestershire sauce
- 2 tsp Dijon mustard
- 350g wide egg noodles
- 1 tbsp all-purpose flour
- 180ml sour cream
- Salt & pepper to taste

Directions

1. Turn the Ninja Foodi on sauté, add oil. When the oil is hot, add the beef, season with salt & pepper. Cook, until browned. Remove from ninja pot and set aside.
2. Add 1 tbsp. butter, add onion, garlic, and mushroom. Cook until soft.
3. Add back beef, add the stock and Worcestershire sauce.
4. Secure lid with valve in seal position. Cook on high pressure for 10 minutes. When time is up, let the pressure release naturally for 5 minutes, then do a quick release.
5. Open the lid and stir. Add the noodles. Stir.
6. Secure lid with valve in seal position. Cook on high pressure for 5 minutes. When time is up, do a quick release.
7. In a medium mixing bowl, mix the flour, butter and sour cream.
8. Open the lid, Turn ninja into saute, add the cream mixture, stir until slightly thicken. Serve

Per Serving: 470kcal
Fat: 29g, Carbohydrates: 15g, Protein: 34g

TACO PASTA

Serving Size: 8 Servings
Total Time: 30 Minutes

Ingredients

- 900g Lean Ground Beef
- 1 package taco seasoning
- 450g pasta
- 950ml water
- 400g tin tomato sauce
- 1 small tin green chilies, (diced)
- Shredded cheese
- Chopped parsley

Directions

1. Turn the ninja in "Sauté" mode. Add the ground beef and cook until well done.
2. Add in the taco seasoning. Add the pasta, water, tomato sauce, and chilies. the liquid should cover the pasta.
3. Secure lid with valve in seal position. Cook on high pressure for 6 minutes.
4. When time is up, do a quick release.
5. Open the lid, stir and let cool for about 5 minutes.
6. Serve topped with cheese and parsley.

Per Serving: 280kcal
Fat: 9g, Carbohydrates: 25g, Protein: 20g

Serving Size
6 Servings

Total Time
25 Minutes

HAMBURGER HELPER

Ingredients

- *1 tbsp. oil*
- *1 large onion, (chopped)*
- *900g lean ground beef*
- *2 garlic cloves, (minced)*
- *1 tbsp. Worcestershire sauce*
- *2 tbsp. tomato paste*
- *950ml beef broth*
- *450g macaroni*
- *250g shredded cheddar cheese*
- *Salt & pepper to taste*
- *Fresh Parmesan Cheese, Optional*

Directions

1. Turn the ninja in "Sauté" mode. Add the oil. When the oil is hot, add onion and garlic and saute until soft.
2. Add beef into the pot and until no pink remains. Season with salt & pepper, then add Worcestershire sauce, tomato paste, beef broth, and macaroni. Mix. (scrape any ground beef off the bottom).
3. Secure lid with valve in seal position. Cook on high for 5 minutes.
4. When time is up, do a quick release.
5. Open the lid and stir. Add cheddar cheese and stir, then serve.

Per Serving: 620kcal
Fat: 20g, Carbohydrates:35g, Protein:25g

Serving Size
6 Servings

Total Time
40 Minutes

SPAGHETTI

Ingredients

- *900g ground beef/turkey, or Italian sausage*
- *1 medium onion, (chopped)*
- *1 tsp. Italian Seasoning*
- *1 tsp. garlic powder*
- *900g dry spaghetti*
- *400g diced tomatoes*
- *2 400g tins crushed tomatoes*
- *750ml water*
- *Salt & pepper to taste*

Directions

1. Turn the ninja in "Sauté" mode. Add ground meat and onions, cook until the meat is browned. Add the spices, stirring to combine. Deglaze with some water and scrape any brown bits off the bottom.
2. Break the spaghetti in half. Layer it on top of the meat mixture.
3. Put the diced tomatoes, crushed tomatoes, and water over the spaghetti.
4. Secure lid with valve in seal position. Cook on high for 7 mins. When time is up, do a quick release.
5. Open the lid and let it sit for 5 mins.
6. Stir and serve.

Per Serving: 530kcal
Fat: 5g, Carbohydrates: 50g, Protein: 25g

3

Seafood Mains

Serving Size
4 Servings

Total Time
25 Minutes

PRAWN FAJITAS

Ingredients

- 900g medium prawn, (tail-off & defrosted)
- 1 red bell pepper, (chopped)
- 1 green bell pepper, (chopped)
- 1 onion, (chopped)
- 2 tbsp. fajita or taco seasoning
- Cooking spray
- Salt & pepper to taste
- Corn/flour tortillas

Directions

1. Spray the ninja basket with cooking spray.
2. Add the peppers, onion, and seasoning to the basket. Mix it together. Then spray evenly with cooking spray. Air Crisp at 200C for 11 minutes.
3. Open the lid and add the prawn. Spray it with cooking spray and mix together. Air Crisp for another 10 minutes.
4. Serve on tortillas.

Per Serving: 88kcal
Fat: 2g, Carbohydrates: 6g, Protein:10g

Serving Size
6 Servings

Total Time
18 Minutes

FISH & CHIPS

Ingredients

- *900g cod fillets*
- *60g flour*
- *30g cornstarch*
- *1 tbsp sugar*
- *120ml cold water*
- *1 egg*
- *100g plain flour*
- *100g breadcrumbs*
- *Salt & pepper to taste*
- *Cooking spray*

For the chips

- *1¼ kg, peeled and cut into 1/2 inch/1.5cm long fries*
- *Salt & pepper to taste*

Directions

1. Soak potatoes in a bowl of cold water for 30 minutes.
2. In a bowl, whisk 60g flour and cornstarch. In another bowl, stir together 100g flour, garlic powder, onion powder, salt, pepper, and baking soda. Pour in cold water and stir to combine. (if too thick add more water)
3. Dredge each fish piece in flour mixture, then in the batter. Place the fish pieces back in the flour mixture to fully coat.
4. Line ninja basket with parchment paper and spray with cooking spray.add fish into basket. (work in batches) Spray tops of fish with cooking spray. Cook at 200°C for 5 minutes. Flip and spray with cooking spray. Air crisp for 4 mins until golden brown.
5. Remove from ninja to a plate and cover with foil. Set aside.
6. drain potatoes and dry them with a towel. spray ninja basket with cooking spray. Place and spray with cooking spray. Air crisp potatoes at 400°F/200°C for 7 minutes. Flip, cook for 7 minutes until golden brown and crispy. Sprinkle with salt and pepper. Serve the fish and chips.

Calories: 211kcal, Carbohydrates: 19g, Protein: 21g, Fat: 5g, Fiber: 1g, Sugar: 1g

Serving Size
6 Servings

Total Time
18 Minutes

CRAB CAKES

Ingredients

- *450g lump crabmeat*
- *60g mayonnaise*
- *30g Panko*
- *60g flour*
- *1 large egg*
- *2 tbsp green onion sliced*
- *1/2 red bell pepper finely diced*
- *1 tbsp Worcestershire sauce*
- *1 tbsp cajun*
- *juice of half lemon*

Directions

1. In a large bowl add crabmeat, mayonnaise, Panko, flour, egg, green onion, bell pepper, Worcestershire sauce, cajun, and lemon juice. Mix and shape into patties.
2. Place in ninja basket. Air crisp at 360°F/182°C for 12 minutes until golden brown

calories: 275kcal, carbohydrates: 13g, protein: 25g, fat: 4g, fiber: 13g, sugar: 1g

Serving Size 4 Servings **Total Time** 25 Minutes

GRILLED PRAWN

Ingredients

- **350g small or medium prawn (peeled, cooked & tail-off)**
- **350g frozen mixed vegetables**
- **Seasoning of choice**
- **Cooking spray**

Directions

1. Spray 4 sheets of foil with cooking spray.
2. Divide the prawn and veggies evenly among the 4 foil packs. Season with a seasoning of your choice, and coat with cooking spray.
3. Preheat the Ninja to high using the grill function.
4. Put the foil packs in the grill, grill on high for 15 mins.
5. Serve over rice.

Per Serving:
CALORIES: 57 TOTAL FAT: 0g SATURATED FAT: 0g TRANS FAT: 0g UNSATURATED FAT: 0g CHOLESTEROL: 2mg SODIUM: 134mg CARBOHYDRATES: 11g FIBER: SUGAR: 3g PROTEIN:

Serving Size 4 Servings

Total Time 15 Minutes

CREAMY CAYENNE PRAWNS

Ingredients

For the marinade
- *500g prawns, (shelled)*
- *2 garlic clove, (minced)*
- *1 tbsp oil*
- *1/5 tbsp butter*

For the sauce
- *2 garlic clove, (minced)*
- *3/4 tsp cayenne*
- *200ml chicken/fish stock*
- *200ml double cream*
- *Salt & pepper to taste*

Directions

1. In a large bowl, mix all the marinade ingredients, put in the prawns and set aside for 10 minutes.
2. Turn the ninja in "Sauté" mode. Add the butter & oil. When the butter & oil is hot, add the prawns, garlic, & cayenne, sauté for 2 mins. Add stock and stir.
3. Secure lid with valve in seal position. Cook on high for 3 mins. When time is up, do a quick release.
4. Open the lid & select saute. Add cream, stir and simmer for a minute.
5. Serve with rice.

Per Serving: 450kcal
Fat: 25g, Carbohydrates: 37g, Protein:9g

Serving Size
4 Servings

Total Time
30 Minutes

SEAFOOD BISQUE

Ingredients

- 2 tbsp. olive oil
- 1 leek, (cut into chunks)
- 1 medium onion, (chopped)
- 1 celery stalk, (chopped)
- 1 tsp. fresh thyme
- 1 tsp. Orange zest
- 230g softened cream cheese
- 700ml chicken stock
- 2 tbsp. tomato paste
- 350 g precooked prawns
- Salt & pepper to taste

Directions

1. Turn the Ninja Foodi on the sauté mode and add the oil. Brown the cubed beef (work in patches), adding more oil as needed. Using a slotted spoon, remove browned beef from the pot and transfer it into a plate.
2. Add garlic and celery to the Ninja, and stir, cook for 1-2 minutes. Return the beef to Ninja. Add in mushrooms and water. Season with salt and black pepper.
3. Secure lid with valve in seal position. Cook on high pressure for 17 minutes. When time is up, do Quick release.
4. Open the lid and add carrots, and potatoes to the pot.
5. Secure lid with valve in seal position and cook again on high pressure for 5 minutes. When time is up, do Quick release.
6. Open the lid and adjust seasoning. Serve immediately.

Per Serving: 254kcal
Fat: 11g, Carbohydrates: 30g, Protein: 21g

Serving Size
4 Servings

Total Time
10 Minutes

THAI POACHED SALMON

Ingredients

- 4 salmon fillets, (120g each)
- 1 (400g) tin coconut milk
- 1 medium lemon (juice and zest)
- 1 lemongrass (peeled, finely grated)
- 1 tbsp. hot sauce
- Handful fresh basil (finely chopped) or 1 tbsp dried basil
- Salt & pepper to taste

Directions

1. Add the salmon fillets, coconut milk, lemon (juice and zest), lemongrass paste, hot sauce, and basil to the Ninja Foodi pot. Then season with salt & pepper.
2. Secure lid with valve in seal position. Cook on High pressure for 3 minutes. When time is up, do a quick release.
3. Open the lid. Adjust seasonings. Serve.

Per Serving: 350kcal
Fat: 26g, Carbohydrates: 7g, Protein: 27g

4

Soups & Stews

Serving Size
6 Servings

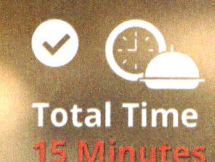

Total Time
15 Minutes

CABBAGE SAUSAGE SOUP

Ingredients

- *100g Butter*
- *250ml Chicken Broth*
- *1 large carrot, (sliced)*
- *1 Head of Cabbage sliced, Core Removed*
- *Salt and Pepper to taste*
- *450g ground sausage browned*

Directions

1. Put all ingredients in the ninja pot.
2. Secure lid with valve in seal position. Cook on high pressure for 8 minutes.
3. When time is up, do a quick release and serve.

Per Serving: 305kcal
Fat: 20g, Carbohydrates: 7g, Protein: 11g

Serving Size: 4 Servings
Total Time: 15 Minutes

CHICKEN ENCHILADA SOUP

Ingredients

- 300g cooked shredded chicken
- 1 packet taco seasoning
- 400g tin black/red beans, drained and rinsed
- 400g tin diced tomatoes with green chilles
- 250g tin mild red enchilada sauce
- 400ml chicken broth
- 180g frozen corn
- 250ml water
- 60ml half and half cream
- 120g shredded cheddar cheese
- Toppings - avocado, sour cream, cilantro, tortilla Strips

Directions

1. Add chicken, taco seasoning, black beans, diced tomatoes, enchilada sauce, chicken broth, corn, and water to the bottom of ninja.
2. Secure lid with valve in seal position. Cook on high pressure for 4 minutes. When time is up, do a quick release.
3. Open the lid, add cream and shredded cheddar cheese. Stir.
4. Serve with toppings of choice.

Per Serving: 360kcal
Fat: 13g, Carbohydrates: 34g, Protein: 29g

Serving Size
6 Servings

Total Time
15 Minutes

CREAMY MUSHROOM SOUP

Ingredients

- *2 tbsp butter*
- *1 tbsp oil*
- *1 onion, (chopped)*
- *4 garlic clove, (minced)*
- *500g mushrooms, (sliced)*
- *1 liter chicken/beef/vegetable stock*
- *1 tsp dried thyme*
- *4 tbsp flour*
- *180ml double cream*
- *Salt & pepper to taste*

Directions

1. Turn the ninja in "Sauté" mode. Add the butter & oil. When the butter & oil is hot, add the onion, garlic, & sauté for 2 mins.
2. Add Mushrooms and saute for 3 mins. Add stock, thyme, and season with salt & pepper.
3. Secure lid with valve in seal position. Cook on high for 5 mins. When time is up, Let the pressure release naturally.
4. Open the lid, select saute and bring the soup to a simmer.
5. In a medium mixing bowl, mix flour and cream. then pour it into the soup, whisking continuously. Season with salt & pepper.
6. Blend the soup, using a hand blender. Transfer into bowls then serve.

Per Serving: 213kcal
Fat: 18g, Carbohydrates: 11g, Protein: 4.7g

Serving Size
5 Servings

Total Time
20 Minutes

CHEESY CAULIFLOWER SOUP

Ingredients

- 3 cloves garlic, (minced)
- 600g raw cauliflower florets
- 750ml vegetable stock
- ¼ tsp. ground mustard powder
- 180g grated cheddar cheese
- 120g double cream
- Salt & pepper to taste

Directions

1. Put the raw garlic, cauliflower, stock, salt, pepper, and mustard powder in the Ninja foodi pot.
2. Secure lid with valve in seal position. Cook on high for 10 mins. When time is up, do a quick release.
3. Open the lid, add the grated cheese and cream. Stir until combined and the cheese is melted.
4. Blend with blender until smooth. Taste and adjust seasoning as desired.
5. Transfer into bowls then serve.

Per Serving: 280kcal
Fat: 22g, Carbohydrates: 5g, Protein: 12g

Serving Size
4 Servings

Total Time
35 Minutes

YELLOW PEA SOUP

Ingredients

- 1 tbsp. olive oil
- 1 onion, (chopped)
- 2 garlic cloves, (minced)
- 1½ tsp. grated fresh ginger
- 225g yellow split peas
- 250ml water
- 650ml vegetable broth
- ¾ tsp. ground saffron
- 80ml full-fat coconut milk or double cream
- Salt & pepper to taste

Directions

1. Turn the Ninja Foodi in "Sauté" mode. Add the oil. When the oil is hot, add the onion and sauté for 2-3 minutes, stirring constantly, or until the onion is translucent and fragrant. Add the ginger and garlic and sauté until fragrant.
2. Press Cancel to stop sauté. Add yellow peas, water, vegetable stock, saffron and salt & black pepper and stir.
3. Secure lid with valve in seal position. Cook on high for 15 mins. When time is up, let the pressure release naturally for 15 minutes, then do a quick release.
4. Open the lid, add the coconut milk or cream. Stir until combined.
5. Transfer into bowls then serve.

Per Serving: 150kcal
Fat: 7g, Carbohydrates: 17g, Protein: 5g

Serving Size
4 Servings

Total Time
15 Minutes

CULLEN SKINK

Ingredients

- 1 onion, (chopped)
- 2 leeks, (chopped)
- 2 potatoes, (peeled & chopped)
- 200g Neeps, (chopped)
- 1 tbsp oil
- 400g Haddock
- 600ml fish stock
- 200ml whole milk
- 2 tsp thyme
- 1 tbsp parsley, (chopped)
- Salt & pepper to taste

Directions

1. Turn the Ninja Foodi in "Sauté" mode. Add the oil. When the oil is hot, add the onion, leek, potatoes, neeps and sauté for 2-3 minutes.
2. Press Cancel to stop sauté. Add Haddock, fis stock, thyme and salt & black pepper and stir.
3. Secure lid with valve in seal position. Cook on high for 8 mins. When time is up, do a quick release.
4. Open the lid, Remove the Haddock, add the milk. Stir until combined. Blend with blender until smooth.
5. Transfer into bowls then serve topped with Haddock and parsley.

Per Serving: 223kcal
Fat: 5g, Carbohydrates: 24g, Protein: 21g

Serving Size
4 Servings

Total Time
10 Minutes

MINESTRONE SOUP

Ingredients

- *3 tbsp oil*
- *1 onion, (chopped)*
- *3 garlic cloves, (minced)*
- *1 celery stalk, (chopped)*
- *1 carrot, (peeled & chopped)*
- *1 tsp dried oregano*
- *1 tsp dried thyme*
- *2 400g tins chopped tomatoes*
- *1 bay leaf*
- *1 liter Vegetable Stock*
- *100g Orzo*
- *Handful baby spinach, (chopped)*
- *4 tbsp grated Parmesan cheese*
- *Salt & pepper to taste*

Directions

1. Turn the ninja in "Sauté" mode. Add the oil. When the oil is hot, add the onion and garlic, sauté for 3 mins.
2. Add carrots, celery, oregano, thyme, tomatoes, bay leaf, stock and orzo.
3. Secure lid with valve in seal position. Cook on high for 2 mins. When time is up, do a quick release.
4. Turn into saute and cook for another 5 mins.
5. Season with salt & pepper. Serve.

Per Serving: 288kcal
Fat: 15g, Carbohydrates: 29g, Protein:9g

Serving Size
8 Servings

Total Time
90 Minutes

CHICKEN NOODLE SOUP

Ingredients

- *1.25 kg chicken thighs, (bone-in & skin on)*
- *1.5 liter chicken stock*
- *2 small yellow onion, (chopped)*
- *4 stalks celery, (chopped)*
- *4 carrots, (peeled & chopped)*
- *2 bay leaves*
- *1 tsp dried thyme*
- *150g dry egg noodles*
- *Salt & pepper to taste*

Per Serving: 400kcal
Fat: 20g, Carbohydrates: 26g, Protein:25g

Directions

1. Add the chicken thighs and chicken stock to the foodi pot.
2. Add bay leaves, and ½ tsp dried thyme, and season with salt & pepper.
3. Secure lid with valve in seal position. Cook on high pressure for 20 minutes.
4. When the time is up, let the pressure release naturally for 5 minutes, then do a quick release.
5. Open the lid, remove the chicken and set aside to cool. Strain broth through a fine mesh strainer. Rinse out the pot to remove any residue.
6. Put back the chicken broth to the inner pot. Add in ½ tsp dried thyme ½ tsp pepper. Add the vegetables and egg noodles.
7. Secure lid with valve in seal position. Cook on high pressure for 1 minute.
8. When the time is up, let the pressure release naturally for 7 minutes, then do a quick release.
9. Remove the chicken skin & bones. Add the chicken meat back to the pot and stir. Serve & Enjoy!

Serving Size
6 Servings

Total Time
30 Minutes

LEEK & POTATO SOUP

Ingredients

- *3 tbsp Butter*
- *1 tbsp Oil*
- *2 large Leeks, (chopped)*
- *1 small Onion, (chopped)*
- *2 Garlic Cloves, (minced)*
- *3 small Potatoes, (Peeled & cubed)*
- *1 liter Chicken/vegetable Stock*
- *100ml Milk*
- *150ml Double Cream*
- *Salt & Pepper to taste*

Directions

1. Turn the ninja in "Sauté" mode. Add the oil. When the oil is hot, add the onion, leeks and garlic, sauté for 3 mins.
2. Add potatoes and saute for another 7 mins. Add the stock and milk. Stir.
3. Secure lid with valve in seal position. Cook on high for 6 mins. When time is up, do a quick release.
4. Open the lid, add cream, season with salt & pepper. Blend the soup, using a hand blender.
5. Transfer into bowls. Serve.

Per Serving: 272kcal
Fat: 18g, Carbohydrates: 24g, Protein:4g

Serving Size: 6 Servings

Total Time: 20 Minutes

CHEESY POTATO SOUP

Ingredients

- **1.36 kg Russet Potatoes, (peeled & into 2cm cubes)**
- **1/4 tsp. nutmeg**
- **60g salted butter**
- **1 medium sweet onion**
- **4 garlic cloves, (minced)**
- **500ml chicken stock**
- **225g cream cheese, (at room temprature)**
- **90g smoked gouda**
- **240g heavy cream**
- **2-3 green onions, (chopped)**
- **Salt & pepper to taste**

Directions

1. Turn the foodi in "Sauté" mode. Add butter. Once hot, add onion. Cook until soft.
2. Add potatoes, garlic cloves, salt, and pepper. Stir and cook for 5 minutes. Add 250ml chicken stock and scrape the bottom of the pot.
3. Secure lid with valve in seal position. Cook on high pressure for 10 minutes.
4. When time is up, let the pressure release naturally for 5 minutes, then do a quick release.
5. Open the lid and use potato masher to break up the potatoes (or use a hand blender) . Add cream cheese and smoked gouda. Stir and allow the cheeses to melt. Add in 125ml chicken broth and 125ml heavy cream and stir. Add more chicken broth & heavy cream if desired consistency is achieved.
6. Add green onions and stir into the soup. Season with salt & pepper to taste. Serve.

Per Serving: 450kcal
Fat: 25g, Carbohydrates: 37g, Protein: 9g

5
Desserts

Serving Size 48 Servings

Total Time 70 Minutes

APPLE BUTTER

Ingredients

- 1 large orange zest
- 2 tbsp orange juice
- 2 kg apples, (peeled, cored & cut into slices)
- 110g brown sugar
- 200gs white sugar
- 1 tsp cinnamon
- ¼ tsp nutmeg
- ¼ tsp salt
- ¼ tsp ground cloves
- ¼ tsp ground cardamom

Directions

1. Add all ingredients to the inner pot of the foodi. Stir.
2. Secure lid with valve in seal position. Cook on High pressure for 10 minutes.
3. When time is up, do a quick release.
4. Open the lid, use an immersion blender to purée the apples.
5. Secure lid with valve in seal position. Set the sear/sauté to medium and cook for 10 minutes. Continue reducing until you get the consistency you like.
6. When you get the desired consistency, turn off the heat and let it cool. Place it in small jars or containers.

Per (1 tbsp) Serving: 47kcal
Fat: 1g, Carbohydrates: 12g, Protein:1g

Serving Size
6 Servings

Total Time
30 Minutes

FLAN

Ingredients

For caramel
- **150g granulated sugar**
- **60ml water**

For the Custard
- **3 large eggs**
- **1 large egg yolk**
- **70g granulated sugar**
- **Dash kosher salt**
- **250ml whole milk**
- **250ml whipping cream**
- **2 tsp vanilla extract**

Directions

1. In a medium saucepan over medium heat, add sugar and water. Cook, gently swirling pan, until sugar is melted and golden brown.
2. Prepare 6 remikens, add 1 tbsp caramel to each ramekin, swirling to coat the bottom. Set ramekins aside
3. In a large mixing bowl, add sugar, egg, egg yolks, salt and vanilla and whisk well.
4. Transfer the mixture into ramekins. Cover with foil
5. Add one cup of water to the bottom of the Ninja pot. Place Trivet. Place the ramekins on the trivet.
6. Secure lid with valve in seal position. Cook on high pressure for 10 minutes, let the pressure release naturally
7. Remove from ninja foodi, chill for 3 hours or overnight. Serve.

Per Serving: 360kcal
Fat: 20g, Carbohydrates: 40g, Protein:7g

Serving Size
4 Servings

Total Time
10 Minutes

EGGY BREAD

Ingredients

- *225ml heavy cream*
- *1 egg beaten*
- *30g powdered sugar*
- *1 tsp cinnamon*
- *8 slices bread*

Directions

1. Preheat Ninja foodi to 200C.
2. Toast bread in batches for bout 4 mins.
3. In a large mixing bowl, mix together remaining ingredients.
4. Once toasted, dip toast into mixture, covering both sides.
5. In batches, Air Crisp at 200c for 5 mins, flipping halfway through cooking time.
6. Serve with fruit and sugar or syrup.

Per Serving: 342kcal
Fat: 18g, Carbohydrates: 20g, Protein: 13g

Serving Size
6 Servings

Total Time
4 hrs 18 minutess

LEMON CURD

Ingredients

- 2 large eggs
- 2 large egg yolks
- 150g granulated sugar
- 125ml fresh lemon juice
- 2 tsp lemon zest
- 1/2 tsp salt
- 5 tbsp unsalted butter, (room temperature)

Directions

1. In a large mixing bowl, add sugar, egg, egg yolks, lemon juice, lemon zest, salt and whisk well.
2. Transfer the mixture into a heatproof glass container that will fit in the Ninja pot. Cover with foil
3. Add one cup of water to the bottom of the Ninja pot. Place Trivet. Place the lemon curd on the trivet.
4. Secure lid with valve in seal position. Cook on high pressure for 3 minutes, when time is up, let the pressure release naturally for 10 minutes, then do a quick release.
5. Remove from ninja foodi, add butter to the lemon curd one tbsp at a time while whisking. Whisk until smooth and creamy.

Per Serving: 182kcal
Fat: 10g, Carbohydrates: 20g, Protein:4g

91

Serving Size
24 Servings

Total Time
2 Hours 10 Minutes

PUMPKIN OATMEAL

Ingredients

- *270g old fashioned oats*
- *50g brown sugar*
- *1/4 tsp baking powder*
- *Handful crushed nuts*
- *1 tsp salt*
- *1 tsp cinnamon*
- *2 tsp pumpkin pie Spice*
- *1 tsp nutmeg*
- *2 eggs*
- *350ml milk*
- *240g pumpkin puree*

Directions

1. In a large mixing bowl, mix all ingredients.
2. Spray the pot of the Ninja with cooking spray.
3. Spread the oatmeal evenly in the bottom of the.
4. Secure lid with valve in seal position. Bake at 165C for 30 mins.
5. Serve with milk.

Per Serving: 212kcal
Fat: 5g, Carbohydrates: 33g, Protein: 8g

Serving Size: 16 Servings

Total Time: 4 Hours

BROWNIES

Ingredients

- 114g salted butter, salted
- 113g dark chocolate chips
- 113g milk chocolate chips
- 200g sugar
- 2 tbsp oil
- 1 tbsp vanilla extract
- 3 large eggs, (slightly beaten)
- 30g unsweetened cocoa powder
- 160g all purpose flour

Directions

1. Turn the foodi on high sear/sauté, add butter. When half melted, add chocolate chips. Stir until chips 75% melted. Turn the Foodi off. Stir.
2. Add sugar and oil, stir until combined. Slowly pour eggs into the batter. Stir until the eggs are incorporated. Add vanilla extract and stir
3. Add cocoa powder and stir to incorporate. Add the flour on 3 times and stir between each addition.
4. Secure lid with valve in seal position. Cook on slow cook function on high for 4 hours.
5. When time is up, do a quick release. Cool and serve.

Per Serving: 330kcal
Fat: 14g, Carbohydrates: 29g, Protein: 3g

Serving Size
6 Servings

Total Time
30 Minutes

COOKIES

Ingredients

- *110g porridge oats*
- *50g smooth salted peanut butter*
- *200g unsweetened apple puree*
- *35g dried cranberries*
- *25g dark chocolate chips*

Directions

1. Line the ninja basket with baking paper
2. In a large mixing bowl, mix all the ingredients until a dough is formed
3. Divide the dough into 6 balls, pressing down to flatten (1cm thick).
4. Put 3 cookies in the Ninja Foodi basket
5. Bake for 12 mins at 180c. Repeat with the other 3 cookies.
6. Let cookies cool for 5 mins. Then serve.

Per Serving: 170kcal
Fat: 7g, Carbohydrates: 21g, Protein:6g

Serving Size
8 Servings

Total Time
50 Minutes

RASPBERRY & ORANGE BREAD PUDDING

Ingredients

- *3 large eggs*
- *70g sugar*
- *1 tsp vanilla extract*
- *Zest of 1 orange*
- *500ml double cream*
- *one loaf challah (cut into 5cm cubes)*
- *30g dried cranberries*
- *125g raspberries*
- *2 tbsp orange juice concentrate*
- *Cooking spray*

Directions

1. Spray a 18cm round cake tin with cooking spray and set aside.
2. In a large mixing bowl, whisk eggs, vanilla, orange zest, orange concentrate and sugar, then add double and mix together.
3. Add the bread cubes, dried cranberries, mix until combined. Fold in the raspberries.
4. Pour the mixture into the prepared tin.
5. Add 250ml water into the Ninja Foodi pot and place a trivet. Place the tin on the trivet.
6. Secure lid with valve in seal position. Cook on High pressure for 30 minutes. When time is up, let it naturally release for 13 minutes then do a quick release.
7. Open the lid, remove the tin to a wire rack, let cool for 10 minutes before serving.

Per Serving: 440kcal
Fat: 26g, Carbohydrates: 37g, Protein: 10g

Serving Size
8 Servings

Total Time
1 Hour 15 Minutes

CHEESECAKE

Ingredients

Crust
- *120g digestive biscuit*
- *50g white sugar*
- *50g brown sugar*
- *6 tbsp melted butter*
- *1 pinch salt*

Cheesecake Filling
- *700g cream cheese, (room temperature)*
- *150g white sugar*
- *1 tbsp vanilla extract*
- *3 eggs*

Directions

1. Mix all the crust ingredients in blender until becomes the consistency of damp sand.
2. Put crust into a 7-Inch Springform cake tin. Pat down the crust using a spatula.
3. Mix all the filling ingredients in blender until combined. Do not over mix.
4. Pour filling into springform pan on top of crust. Tap the tin on the counter to eliminate extra air. Cover tin with foil. Cover the bottom and sides too.
5. Add 500ml water into the Ninja Foodi pot and place a trivet. Place the tin on the trivet.
6. Secure lid with valve in seal position. Cook on High pressure for 42 minutes. When time is up, let it naturally release for 26 minutes then do a quick release.
7. Open the lid, remove the tin, separate cheesecake from sides of tin.
8. Let it cool on counter for an hour and then refrigerate for at least 2 hours.
9. Remove cheesecake from tin and serve!

Per Serving: 570kcal
Fat: 40g, Carbohydrates: 45g, Protein: 8g

Serving Size
12 Servings

Total Time
35 Minutes

MINI LEMON PIES

Ingredients

- *2 eggs*
- *Juice & zest of 1 lemon*
- *40g plain flour*
- *60g melted butter*
- *200g sweetened condensed milk*
- *125ml milk*

Directions

1. Grease and flour a 6 silicone mini muffin tin.
2. In a large mixing bowl, whisk all the ingredients until combined.
3. Divide the batter into prepared muffin tin.
4. Put muffin tin in the Ninja Foodi basket.
5. Air crisp for 6 mins at 160C. Repeat with the remaining pies.
6. Remove from Ninja, Let pies cool for 5 mins. Then serve.

Per Serving: 117kcal
Fat: 6.5g, Carbohydrates: 12g, Protein:3g

Serving Size
4 Servings

Total Time
48 Minutes

APPLE CRUMBLE

Ingredients

- 850g Granny Smith apples, (peeled & chopped into 2cm cubes)
- 1 1/2 tbsp cornflour
- 1 tsp lemon juice
- 120ml water
- 40g white sugar

Topping

- 60ml water
- 50g brown sugar
- 75g flour
- 50g rolled oats
- 25g white sugar
- 100g unsalted butter
- 1 tsp ground cinnamon
- 1/4 tsp salt
- Vanilla ice cream

Directions

1. In a medium mixing bowl, mix cornflour, 60ml water, lemon juice, and sugar, then add apples and toss.
2. Put apples into a baking dish, cover with foil.
3. Pour 120ml water into the pot, and place the baking dish on the trivet, making sure trivet is in the lower position. Secure lid with valve in seal position.
4. Cook on High for 8 minutes.
5. In a mixing bowl, mix all topping ingredients until combined.
6. When time is up, do a quick release.
7. Remove foil and spread topping evenly over the apples. Close lid. Select air crisp at 180°C, for 10 minutes. Rotate halfway through cooking.
8. When time is up, , remove from pot and serve with vanilla ice cream.

Per Serving: 600kcal
Fat: 22g, Carbohydrates: 50g, Protein: 5g

Serving Size
6 Servings

Total Time
10 Minutes

RICE PUDDING

Ingredients

- **220g Arborio rice**
- **375ml water**
- **500ml whole milk , divided**
- **100g granulated sugar**
- **2 egg whites**
- **80g raisins**
- **½ tsp. vanilla**
- **½ tsp. cinnamon plus more for topping (optional)**
- **Whipped cream (optional)**

Directions

1. Put the rice and water in the Ninja Foodi pot.
2. Secure lid with valve in seal position. Cook on High pressure for 3 minutes. When time is up, do a quick release.
3. Open the lid, turn Ninja into saute mood, Add 250ml milk and sugar to the rice.
4. In a small mixing bowl, combine the remaining milk and the egg whites, whisk lightly.
5. Add the milk and egg mixture, raisins, vanilla, and cinnamon to the Ninja Foodi pot.
6. Stir constantly until the rice pudding begins to boil and thicken. Add more milk until the pudding reaches the desired consistency.
7. Serve hot or cold topped with whipped cream and cinnamon.

Per Serving: 280kcal
Fat: 3g, Carbohydrates: 50g, Protein:6g

Serving Size
8 Servings

Total Time
45 Minutes

BLACKBERRY COBBLER

Ingredients

- *4 tbsp melted unsalted butter*
- *100g self-rising flour*
- *50g sugar*
- *1/2 tsp salt*
- *1 tbsp lemon zest*
- *125ml lemon-lime soda*
- *170g blackberries*
- *Cooking spray*

Directions

1. In a medium mixing bowl, add flour, melted butter sugar, salt, lemon zest, lemon/lime soda and vanilla extract. Whisk until combined batter formed.
2. Spray a baking dish with cooking spray. Add batter to the baking dish, add blackberries on top. Cover with foil.
3. Put the baking dish in ninja.
4. Select air crisp at 160°C, for 20. Remove foil and air crisp for more 15 minutes until golden and cooked through.
5. Remove from ninja, let set for 15 minutes, then serve.

Per Serving: Calories: 130kcal | Carbohydrates: 19g | Protein: 2g | Fat: 6g | Fiber: 2g | Sugar: 9g

Serving Size
6 Servings

Total Time
40 Minutes

STRAWBERRY SCONES

Ingredients

- 180g plain flour
- 50g granulated sugar
- 1 ¼ tsp baking powder
- ¼ tsp baking soda
- ¼ tsp salt
- 6 tbsp cold unsalted butter, (cut into small pieces)
- 120ml buttermilk
- 4 large strawberries, (diced)
- Cooking spray

Directions

1. In a large mixing bowl, sift flour, baking soda, baking powder, and salt. Mix and set aside.
2. Add butter to dry ingredients. Use a fork to mash the butter into the flour mixture. Add buttermilk and mix until a rough dough formed.
3. Add strawberries into the dough and gently mix without squishing the strawberries.
4. Form the dough into a circle and then flatten to 2-cm thick.
5. Add scone in ninja foodi.
6. Air crisp at 175C for 18 minutes.
7. Remove from ninja. Allow to cool then serve.

Per Serving: Calories: 300kcal | Carbohydrates: 40g | Protein: 4g | Fat: 14g | Fiber: 1g | Sugar: 15g

Serving Size
8 Servings

Total Time
25 Minutes

BISCUITS

Ingredients

- 240g all-purpose flour
- 3 tsps baking powder
- 1/2 tsp salt
- 7 tbsp cold butter cut into little squares
- 240ml cold milk
- 2 tbsp melted butter to brush on the tops

Directions

1. In a large bowl, Mix flour, baking powder and salt. Cut in the cold butter until the mixture resembles gravel. Add milk and stir to form a dough. Do not over mix.
2. With a spoon, scoop out 10 biscuits.
3. Place biscuits, spaced apart, in ninja basket. You may need to cook in 2 batches.
4. Air crisp at 205°C for 8 minutes, then open the lid and brush on the melted butter. Continue cooking until lightly golden brown on top, for 2 more minutes.

Calories: 197kcal | Carbohydrates: 12g | Protein: 3g | Fat: 111g | Sodium: 344mg | Fiber: 1g | Sugar: 1g

Serving Size
6 Servings

Total Time
25 Minutes

BREAD PUDDING

Ingredients

- *100g bread cubes*
- *1 egg*
- *150ml heavy cream*
- *1/2 tsp vanilla extract*
- *50g sugar*
- *50g chocolate chips*
- *Cooking spray*

Directions

1. Spray a 18-cm round baking dish with cooking spray.
2. Add bread cubes to the baking dish, sprinkle chocolate chips on top.
3. In a medium mixing bowl, add heavy cream, egg, sugar, and vanilla extract. Whisk until combined.
4. Pour egg mixture over the bread cubes. Set aside for 5 minutes.
5. Put the baking dish in ninja.
6. Air crisp at 175C for 15 minutes, until cooked through.
7. Remove from ninja, serve.

Per Serving: Calories: 375kcal | Carbohydrates: 50g | Protein: 9g | Fat: 14g | Fiber: 4g | Sugar: 18g

Serving Size
4 Servings

Total Time
15 Minutes

BANANA BUNDT CAKE

Ingredients

For the cake
- 2 bananas
- 1 egg
- 150g sugar
- 70ml oil
- 1 tsp vanilla extract
- 120g plain flour
- 1/2 tsp cinnamon
- 1 tsp baking powder
- 1/2 tsp baking soda
- 1/2 tsp salt

Cream cheese icing
- 2 tbsp butter, softened
- 60g cream cheese softened
- 100g powdered sugar
- 1 tsp vanilla extract
- 2 tbsp heavy cream

Directions

For the cake:
1. In a large bowl, mash the bananas, then add the egg. Mix. Add the sugar, oil, and vanilla extract and mix until combined.
2. Sift in the dry ingredients over the banana/egg mixture. Fold the dry ingredients into the batter.
3. Pour the batter into a mini bundt pan. Add into ninja.
4. Air crisp at 160°c for 14 minutes.
5. Rotate the 180° and air crisp for 15 minutes.
6. Remove from Ninja. Let the cake cool completely.

For the icing:
1. Microwave butter & cream cheese for 7 to 10 seconds then stir and microwave for another 7 seconds.
2. Add the powdered sugar and vanilla. Stir until smooth. Whisk in the cream.
3. Drizzle the icing over the cake and serve.

Per Serving: **CALORIES: 291,** FAT: 13g, CARBOHYDRATES: 42g, FIBER: 1g, SUGAR: 29g, PROTEIN: 3g

Serving Size
5 Servings

Total Time
25 Minutes

STRAWBERRY RHUBARB CRUMBLES

Ingredients

- 450g strawberries, (hulled & halved)
- 450g rhubarb, trimmed & cut into 1.5cm pieces
- 50g + 3 tbsp sugar, divided
- 1 tbsp cornstarch
- 6 tbsp unsalted butter, cut into small cubes
- 100g plain flour
- ¼ tsp salt
- 30g almonds, chopped
- Cooking spray

Directions

1. Spray small ramekins with cooking spray and set aside.
2. In a large mixing bowl, add strawberries, rhubarb, 50g sugar and cornstarch. Mix.
3. In another bowl, add the butter and flour, rubbing together with hands until they resemble breadcrumbs. Then, add 3 tbsp sugar, salt & almonds and mix the mixture together.
4. Divide the fruit mixture among the ramekins and top with the crumble mixture. Put in Ninja and air crisp at 175°C for 21 minutes.

Per Serving: Calories: 280kcal | Carbohydrates: 38g | Protein: 4g | Fat: 14g | Fiber: 4g | Sugar: 18g

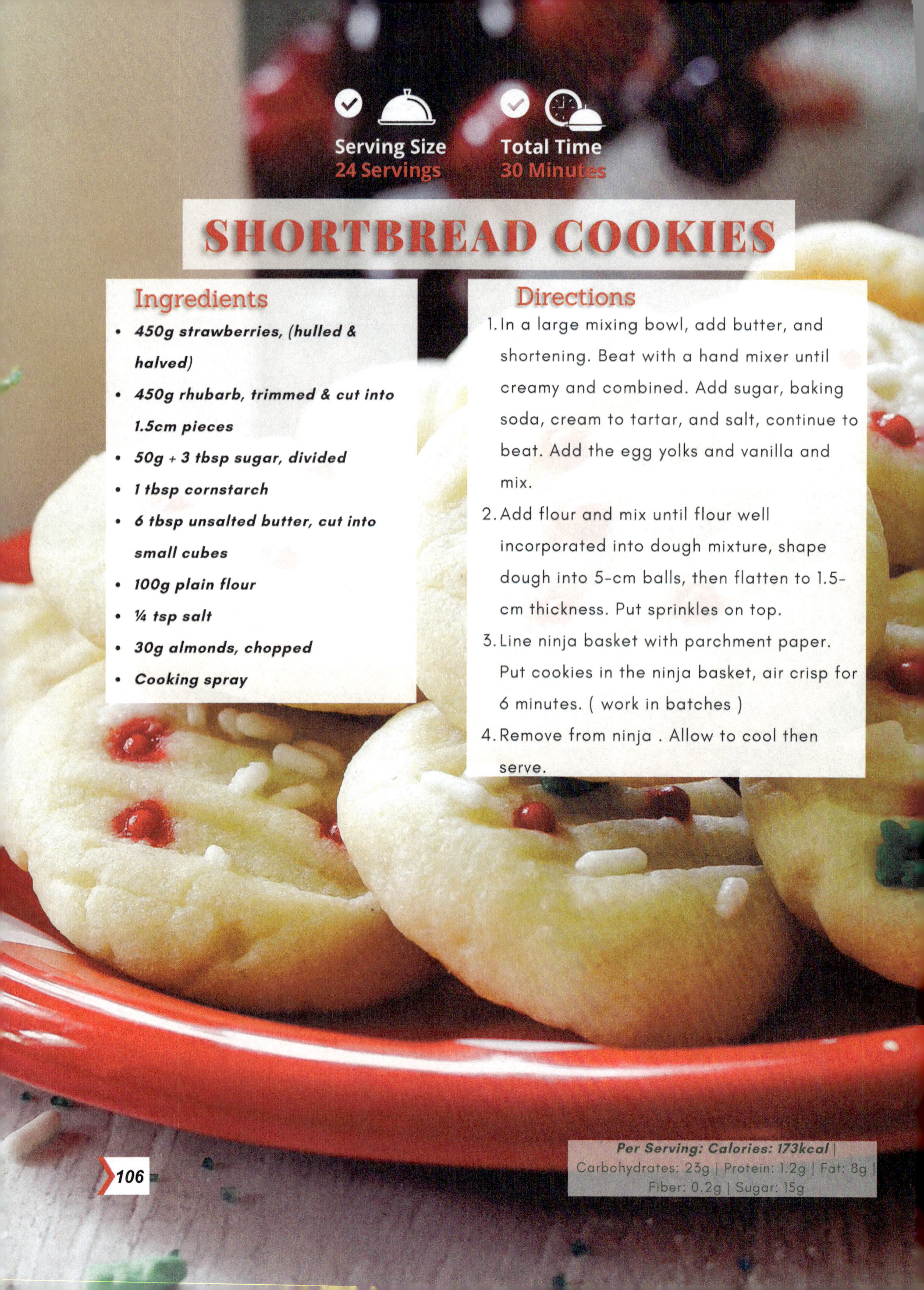

Serving Size
24 Servings

Total Time
30 Minutes

SHORTBREAD COOKIES

Ingredients

- 450g strawberries, (hulled & halved)
- 450g rhubarb, trimmed & cut into 1.5cm pieces
- 50g + 3 tbsp sugar, divided
- 1 tbsp cornstarch
- 6 tbsp unsalted butter, cut into small cubes
- 100g plain flour
- ¼ tsp salt
- 30g almonds, chopped
- Cooking spray

Directions

1. In a large mixing bowl, add butter, and shortening. Beat with a hand mixer until creamy and combined. Add sugar, baking soda, cream to tartar, and salt, continue to beat. Add the egg yolks and vanilla and mix.
2. Add flour and mix until flour well incorporated into dough mixture, shape dough into 5-cm balls, then flatten to 1.5-cm thickness. Put sprinkles on top.
3. Line ninja basket with parchment paper. Put cookies in the ninja basket, air crisp for 6 minutes. (work in batches)
4. Remove from ninja . Allow to cool then serve.

Per Serving: Calories: 173kcal | Carbohydrates: 23g | Protein: 1.2g | Fat: 8g | Fiber: 0.2g | Sugar: 15g

Serving Size
3 Servings

Total Time
15 Minutes

BLUEBERRY MUFFIN

Ingredients

- *1 egg*
- *65g sugar*
- *80 ml oil*
- *2 tbsp water*
- *¼ tsp vanilla extract*
- *1 tsp lemon zest*
- *80g flour*
- *½ tsp baking powder*
- *Pinch of salt*
- *75g blueberries*

Directions

1. In a bowl, Mix the wet ingredients and the zest. Set aside.
2. In a smaller bowl whisk the dry ingredients. Add the dry ingredients to the wet ingredients.
3. Spray 3 silicon muffin liners with cooking spray and set aside. Scoop batter into papers with an ice cream scoop.
4. Air crisp at 180°C. for 17 minutes

Calories: 39kcal | Carbohydrates: 15g | Protein: 2g | Fat: 3g | fiber 11g. Sugar: 0g

Printed in Great Britain
by Amazon